LABOR MIGRATION AND ECONOMIC GROWTH

A Case Study of Puerto Rico

M.I.T. MONOGRAPHS IN ECONOMICS

LABOR MIGRATION
AND ECONOMIC GROWTH
A Case Study of Puerto Rico

STANLEY L. FRIEDLANDER

THE M.I.T. PRESS

Massachusetts Institute of Technology
Cambridge, Massachusetts, and London, England

Acknowledgments

I wish to acknowledge my indebtedness to the members of my thesis committee: Professor Charles A. Myers, Evsey D. Domar, and Robert Evans Jr., for their cooperation, guidance, and valuable suggestions, which contributed to the improvement of the manuscript.

I want to thank Professor Abraham Siegel for his advice in the formulation of the research project and Professor Franklin Fisher for his help with some of the conceptual and statistical problems.

The research would not have been possible without the cooperation and data supplied by the Commonwealth of Puerto Rico's Departments of Health and Labor, the Puerto Rican Planning Board, and the Division of Migration in New York City.

I want to acknowledge my appreciation to the Department of Economics for its financial support of the dissertation research.

The form and presentation of the manuscript has been improved by the excellent editing and typing of Miss Beatrice Rogers.

To my parents, who have been a constant source of encouragement and inspiration throughout the years of my education, I want to express my sincere gratitude.

To my wife, Naomi, who has endured the rigors of graduate student life, goes my deepest appreciation. Her conscientious work preparing the bibliography and footnotes and editing and proofreading contributed to the completion of the thesis. But more important, her patience, encouragement, hard work, and understanding have been important factors in all of my work.

STANLEY L. FRIEDLANDER

August 1965

Contents

Tables

Figures

1

Introduction

Poverty or Progress

Economic backwardness and rapid population growth plague many countries today. More than two thirds of the world's population live under intolerable conditions of hunger and poverty. The rising aspirations of these people have placed great pressure on their leaders to find the methods, institutions, and economic systems that can best produce rapid economic growth.

Nations representing the alternative systems of communism and capitalism constantly struggle — using loans, grants, technical assistance, gifts, private and public foreign investments — to stimulate the economic growth of these less developed countries and, in turn, to convince their leaders of the advantages of operating under one or the other economic system. There is very little doubt that the economic decisions made by the leaders of the uncommitted and underdeveloped nations will be one of the basic determinants in the future balance of world power. It is for this reason that it is imperative to examine every method that may help raise the standard of living of the people in many underdeveloped nations, on either humanitarian or self-interest grounds.

During the past twenty-five years the world has experienced a significant demographic revolution. Advances in medical science and the establishment of comprehensive health programs initiated by international agencies and national governments have resulted in a sharp reduction in the mortality rates in many countries throughout the world. The existence of high birth rates and the sharp decreases in the death rate have resulted in a rapid growth of population in many already densely populated, less developed countries. This demographic revolution has placed an even greater burden on many of these underdeveloped nations struggling to achieve economic progress.

1

The Search for Alternatives

The factors contributing to subsistence levels of living and economic backwardness usually include (1) lack of capital accumulation, (2) unskilled and uneducated labor force, (3) absence of entrepreneurs, (4) poor natural resource base, (5) rapidly growing population, (6) backward technology and equipment, (7) unstable governments, and (8) absence of economic motivation and attitudes of achievement and desire for material accumulation. The literature of economic development has focused primarily on capital formation as the crucial variable in the process of economic growth. The major types of aid given by the advanced industrialized nations have been technical and capital assistance. Although this aid has been useful in stimulating the growth of output, rapid population growth has in many cases absorbed much of the gain. Thus, instead of observable improvements in the standard of living and income per capita of the population, the growth of output has been used to support and feed the growing numbers of people.

Two potential solutions are available: (*a*) an all-out effort to reduce the birth rate, quickly and significantly, and (*b*) emigration. It is often quite difficult to effectively reduce the birth rate during the early stages of economic development. The majority of the population does not have the attitudes, desires, motivations, knowledge, and income levels that facilitate significant changes in fertility patterns. The second alternative, emigration, may be a potential solution to the population growth problem of certain countries. At the present time political and legal barriers prevent the free movement of many of the people of the world, although some countries, particularly in South America, have open-door policies favoring immigration. In the future, it may be desirable for other countries to re-examine and revise their restrictive immigration policies if two countries can derive positive benefits from a more efficient allocation of labor due to increased freedom of movement of their populations.

Role of Emigration

The major objective of this study is to analyze the effects of emigration on the economic growth of an underdeveloped country.

A United Nations survey report on the determinants and consequences of population growth has stated

Emigration has . . . been favored and in some cases held to be an economic necessity for countries where the population was considered to be above the optimum. This argument has been advanced most often and most forcefully with reference to densely populated agricultural countries and to semi-industrialized countries such as Japan and Italy, where large rural populations are employed at a low level of productivity on relatively small areas of cultivable land.[1]

On the other hand, many demographers contend that historically emigration has not been a useful method of reducing population growth. A representative view has been expressed by Henry Pratt Fairchild:

In short, reliance on emigration as a means of relieving population pressure has hitherto proved almost a complete failure, whether officially administered or left to the initiative of the individual migrants. It has practically never reduced the home population sufficiently to provide for a significant improvement in the level of living.[2]

There are some important exceptions to this general judgment. The most notable is the case of Ireland in the two decades between 1840 and 1860, when there was large-scale emigration to the United States. During the peak decade, 1851–1861, almost one sixth of the Irish population emigrated. The effect on Ireland's population pattern was crucial: the Irish population was 8,175,000 in 1841 and almost half that, 4,390,000, in 1911.[3] Moreover, the fact that emigration did not alter the population of many countries in the past does not preclude the possibility of its doing so today. Whether emigration can effect changes in a country's population growth and structure will in part determine its effect on the country's economic development. A major part of my research is devoted to answering this important question.

Insights from the Literature

From the economist's perspective, there is a diversity of opinion and theoretical analysis on the usefulness of emigration. An out-

---

[1] United Nations, Department of Social Affairs, Population Division, *The Determinants and Consequences of Population Trends*, Population Study No. 17 (New York: United Nations, 1953), p. 288. This report contains an exhaustive bibliography and complete summary on studies of migration.

[2] Henry Pratt Fairchild, *People, the Quantity and Quality of Population* (New York: Henry Holt, 1939), p. 235.

[3] Brinley Thomas, *Migration and Economic Growth* (London: University Press of Cambridge, 1954), pp. 72–82.

standing piece of theoretical work by Arthur Lewis[4] contends that the existence of excess supplies of labor can be employed as an important device by which economic growth can be stimulated. However, other economists, particularly Paul Rosenstein-Rodan,[5] have emphasized the importance of eliminating the excess disguised unemployment in the agricultural sector of underdeveloped economies in order to stimulate economic growth. In one of the recent theoretical works on this subject, Fei and Ranis contend that the key to successful economic development is the reallocation of labor from the less productive agricultural sector to the more dynamic and productive industrial sector of the economy.

A distinctive feature of the underdeveloped economy with labor surplus is the predominance of an agricultural sector characterized by widespread disguised unemployment and high rates of population growth, side by side with a small but growing industrial sector and an acute shortage of capital. In such a dualistic (*i.e.*, two-sector) setting, the heart of the development problem lies in the gradual shifting of the economy's center of gravity from the agricultural to the industrial sector through labor reallocation. . . . Moreover, in countries exhibiting the above characteristics, labor reallocation must be rapid enough to swamp massive population increases if the economy's center of gravity is to be shifted over time. . . . If the combined forces of capital accumulation and innovation yield a rate of labor reallocation in excess of the rate of population growth, the economy may be considered to be successful in the development effort in the sense that the center of gravity is continuously shifted towards the industrial sector.[6]

The major thesis of Fei and Ranis is that labor-using or capital-saving investment is a necessity in order to rapidly shift the labor supply into the industrial sector. In contrast, Galenson and Leibenstein[7] have contended that it is crucial to invest in capital intensive

[4] Arthur Lewis, "Economic Development with Unlimited Supplies of Labor," *Manchester School of Economic and Social Studies,* Vol. XXII (May 1954), pp. 139–191.

[5] Paul Rosenstein-Rodan, "Problems of Industrialization of Eastern and South-Eastern Europe," *Economic Journal,* Vol. LIII (June 1943), pp. 202–211.

[6] John C. H. Fei and Gustav Ranis, "Innovation, Capital Accumulation, and Economic Development," *American Economic Review,* Vol. LIII (June 1963), pp. 283–284.

[7] Walter Galenson and Harvey Leibenstein, "Investment Criteria, Productivity and Economic Development," *Quarterly Journal of Economics,* Vol. LXIX (1955), pp. 343–369.

industries possessing advanced technology in order to obtain rapid increases in productivity in the industrial sector of the economy. The controversy among economists and demographers as to the effects of emigration on population and economic growth continues. Can emigration reduce the population problem and concomitantly eliminate excess supplies of labor and aid in the attraction of capital intensive high productivity industries?

Brinley Thomas[8] has written an excellent and comprehensive analysis of migration and economic growth of the Atlantic economy.[9] Unfortunately, the study is primarily confined to the effect of emigration on the economic growth of the United States and Great Britain. The extreme differences in structure, form, and conditions of these two economies in the nineteenth century compared to present-day underdeveloped, densely populated economies severely limits the applicability of the findings and generalizations presented in Thomas's work.

The United Nations in an exhaustive survey of the literature on emigration concluded that

> Studies concerned with the economic and social effect of international and internal migration have been limited largely to the industrialized countries. The available literature dealing with effects of emigration from a densely populated, economically underdeveloped country remains largely speculative.[10]

The absence of information and scientific analysis about the effect of emigration on economic growth and population of underdeveloped nations has provided the opportunity for a great deal of controversy and opinionated debate. But, after all is said, very little is known about the actual effects of emigration on the process of economic growth. It is the specific purpose of this research to analyze, theoretically and empirically, the effects of emigration on economic growth of underdeveloped, densely populated countries.

With the potential importance of emigration, it is natural to

---

[8] Brinley Thomas, *op. cit.* Chapter 1 of this book succinctly reviews the early nineteenth-century debates and literature on the pros and cons of emigration and colonization from Great Britain to the colonies.

[9] *Ibid.* The study includes an analysis of the effects of migration on the countries bordering the North Atlantic, specifically United States, Canada, Ireland, Great Britain, and Sweden.

[10] United Nations, *op. cit.*, p. 314.

inquire why there has not been any empirical analysis of the effect of emigration. One of the major reasons has been the absence of large-scale emigration from underdeveloped countries in recent years because of restrictive immigration laws prohibiting movement into many of the industrialized nations. Another problem has been the lack of reliable data either on the economics of underdeveloped countries or on the type, size, and characteristics of the migration.

Why Puerto Rico?

Fortunately, Puerto Rico is an exception; a large-scale emigration of Puerto Ricans to the United States occurred during the postwar period, 1945–1963. Even more important, reliable data are available on the variables affecting the economic growth of Puerto Rico and on the size and characteristics of the migration. These two factors provide an excellent setting for an empirical analysis of the effect of emigration on the economic growth of Puerto Rico.

Prior to 1940, Puerto Rico was a typical underdeveloped area. The island had an agricultural economy, dominated by one major crop — sugar. The conditions on the island were sufficiently intolerable to earn the label of "the poorhouse of the Caribbean." Between 1926 and 1939 income per capita had stagnated at a level of approximately $100. Population density was extremely high, limited amounts of cultivatable land existed, the natural resource base on the island was extremely poor. The illiteracy rate was very high, population growth was close to 2.0 per cent per annum, investments and savings were negligible, and modern technology and desirable economic attitudes and motivations were lacking. The outlook for raising the standard of living of the population was extremely pessimistic. The tremendous imbalance of population and resources seemed impossible to overcome. A demographic revolution on the island, commencing in 1940, intensified these intolerable conditions. A sharp reduction in the death rate, combined with one of the world's highest birth rates, brought rapid population growth. Yet, despite all the pessimism and hopelessness, a remarkable transformation occurred. Puerto Rico moved from poverty and depression to a dynamic, progressive, industrialized island economy within a short period of twenty years.

Limitations of the Puerto Rican Experience

The remarkably successful development of the Puerto Rican economy has attracted thousands of leaders and advisers from many other underdeveloped nations seeking to learn the techniques and lessons of the Puerto Rican experience. It is important that these leaders and advisers recognize the implicit limitations of imitating Puerto Rican methods and techniques of economic planning and growth. The transfer value of the Puerto Rican experience may be limited. The unique relationship of Puerto Rico and the United States provides one large internal market, similar in certain respects to the common market. A common currency is used, there are no tariff barriers, and Puerto Ricans are citizens of the United States with freedom to enter and leave the continental boundaries of the United States at any time. In addition, Puerto Ricans receive large grants of federal aid from the United States without contributing taxes to the United States government. The government of Puerto Rico, under its unique commonwealth status arrangement with the United States, does not have to allocate funds for national defense. Furthermore, large amounts of United States private capital have flowed into Puerto Rico in the last twenty years, providing a substantial portion of investment funds to stimulate their rapid economic growth. The close political and economic relationship between the United States and Puerto Rico thus limits the applicability of the findings of this research to other underdeveloped nations. In fact, the unique relationship was responsible for the absence of immigration barriers and allowed for the large-scale movement of the Puerto Rican population. Given the current status of restrictive immigration policies by many of the developed countries, it is unlikely that mass movements of populations across national boundaries will occur in the near future.

Although the Puerto Rican experience is unique, it does not have to remain so, providing other countries study and evaluate the role of emigration as an important variable in the economic development process. All underdeveloped countries are constantly seeking closer economic ties with the more advanced countries in the area of increased trade, capital and technical assistance, and foreign aid. If emigration can help stimulate the economic development of these countries and is mutually beneficial for both the sending and receiving countries, then changes in immigration policies are needed. Careful analysis and practical plans should be undertaken to evaluate the usefulness and desirability of emigration in each case.

Many of the benefits from Puerto Rico's association with the United States can be recognized and accounted for directly by those desiring to imitate Puerto Rico's experience. But the precise effects of emigration on economic development are more difficult to recognize since there has been no adequate analysis of its role. Thus this research has the additional goal of providing information to other countries on the role of emigration in Puerto Rico's economic growth and the potential it may have for stimulating economic progress in other underdeveloped countries.

Preview

The study is divided into two sections. The first — comprising Chapter 2 — is a theoretical analysis of the potential role of emigration on the economic growth of an underdeveloped country experiencing rapid population growth. It is impossible to analyze the effect of emigration on the economic growth of a country without specifying the conditions existing in the economy at the time of emigration and the size and characteristics of the migration. This analysis is confined to the effect of migration on an economy that not only experiences rapid population growth but has limited capital investment and large-scale disguised unemployment in the agricultural sector and open unemployment in the industrial sector.

The second section of my study attempts to analyze the role of emigration in the economic growth of Puerto Rico. It would be impossible to obtain an exact quantitative estimate of the effect of emigration on the growth of either output or income per capita in Puerto Rico without constructing a complex and somewhat unrealistic model of the Puerto Rican economy. An attempt to make *ceteris paribus* assumptions about certain variables in the economy and to estimate what effect emigration had on other variables separately would have been equally unrealistic. Therefore, instead of using either method, the approach selected was to examine the impact of emigration on several crucial variables that affect the economic growth process.

Emigration usually has its most significant impact on population. Chapter 3 analyzes the effect of emigration on the size, growth, and structure of the Puerto Rican population. A study of the relationship between economic growth and fertility rates of Puerto Rico is also included in this chapter.

Emigration affects not only population, it has a definite impact on the supply and quality of the labor force. Chapter 4 examines the occupational characteristics of the migrants and the size of the migrants' labor force and analyzes its effect on the size and quality of the Puerto Rican labor force. The chapter concludes with an analysis of the effect of migration on unemployment in the island.

A great many studies have attempted to explore the push and pull factors responsible for the fluctuation in the movement of labor internally and internationally. The type of occupational characteristics possessed by the migrants can determine whether emigration exerts a positive or negative effect on the economic growth of an economy. Chapter 5 is concerned with the economic factors determining these characteristics. A crucial migration hypothesis advanced in the theoretical chapter, regarding the determination of the occupational structure of the emigrants, is examined with data from the Puerto Rican migration experience.

Migration has a definite impact on the quality of the labor force, directly as various types of occupations enter and leave it, and indirectly as the quality and amount of education received by future labor force members increases. Chapter 6 shows how the improvement in the quality of the labor force influenced the growth of output and productivity in the Puerto Rican economy.

The final chapter contains a summary of the major empirical findings concerning the effect of emigration on the Puerto Rican economy. Policy recommendations and the implications of the role of migration in the future growth of Puerto Rico are discussed. The study concludes with a discussion of the limitations and benefits of emigration as an aid to economic growth in other underdeveloped, densely populated countries.

2

A Theoretical Analysis
of the Effects of Emigration
on Economic Development

Introduction

The "population explosion" has compelled many economists to focus greater attention on the economic significance of rapid population growth. The classical school of economics under the influence of Malthus and Ricardo placed great emphasis on the growth of population as an integral aspect of economic growth. Until recently, most neoclassical growth theories have treated population growth as an exogenous variable.

The recent literature in the field of economic development indicates a return to the classical treatment of population growth, and a number of significant theoretical analyses[1] have incorporated population growth as an endogenous variable, affecting and being affected by economic growth. This treatment of population is desirable and justified because it provides a more realistic picture

[1] Robert M. Solow, "A Contribution to the Theory of Economic Growth," *Quarterly Journal of Economics*, Vol. LXX, No. 1 (February 1956), p. 91; R. R. Nelson, "A Theory of the Low-Level Equilibrium Trap," *American Economic Review*, Vol. XLVI, No. 5 (December 1956), pp. 894–908; W. Arthur Lewis, "Economic Development with Unlimited Supplies of Labor," *The Manchester School of Economics and Social Studies*, Vol. XXII (May 1954), pp. 139–191; Harvey Leibenstein, Economic Backwardness and Economic Growth (New York: John Wiley & Sons, 1957); Everett E. Hagen, "Population and Economic Growth," *American Economic Review* (June 1959), p. 310.

of the difficult problem of achieving significant improvements in the standard of living for the population in many economically underdeveloped countries.

This chapter constructs a theoretical framework in which the effect of emigration on the economic growth process can be analyzed. The framework consists of a series of successive modifications moving from a simple model to a more complete and complex set of interrelated hypotheses. The first step is a modified version of the low-level income trap, originally proposed independently by Professors Nelson and Leibenstein.[2] The model describes the mechanism by which rapid population growth prevents increases in the growth of output resulting in a stagnating economy at a low-level subsistence per capita income. The second step describes two possible methods by which the income trap can be broken: (a) investment of foreign capital, and (b) large-scale emigration. The third step shows how both factors of production, capital inflow and labor outflow, can be utilized simultaneously. The fourth and final step consists of major modifications of the original hypotheses to provide a more complete and realistic framework.

The interaction of economic and demographic variables is affected by the stage of economic development existing in a country. During the actual process of economic development the relationships between the economic and demographic variables may change considerably. At early stages of economic development, the growth of income may stimulate rapid population growth which, in turn, may retard the future rate of economic growth. In contrast, rapid population growth may be a significant factor in stimulating investment and economic growth in more developed but stagnating economies. The theoretical framework presented in this chapter is confined to the relationships and interactions of economic and demographic variables during the early stages of economic development, from the inception of economic growth to the stage of self-sustained growth.

The model is applicable to the analysis of emigration in areas or countries that exhibit certain preconditions: (1) population pressure on existing scarce natural resources; (2) a predominantly traditional agricultural economy operated under labor-intensive methods; (3) full utilization of all cultivable land areas; (4) an excess supply of labor in the agricultural sector, that is, disguised

---

[2] Nelson, *op. cit.* and Leibenstein, *op. cit.*

unemployment, or open unemployment in the industrial sector; (5) negligible amounts of net savings; and (6) low level of income per capita. These conditions in differing degrees can be found in many countries in Asia, Central America, and the islands in the Caribbean area. Under these conditions rapid population growth presents a serious and difficult obstacle for improving the standard of living of the population. The rate of population growth will determine, in part, the rate of increase in per capita income during the early stages of economic growth and whether the economy stagnates at a low-level per capita income. Emigration can have a powerful positive effect on the reduction of population growth and the stimulation of the growth of output enabling an economy to overcome stagnation at low levels of per capita income and stimulate even more rapid increases in the per capita income. The following series of steps analyzes the theoretical effect of emigration on the economic growth of a country fulfilling the preconditions just described.

A Low-Level Income Trap

Leibenstein's and Nelson's theoretical works on the interaction of economic and demographic variables provide a useful foundation on which to build a framework to analyze the effect of emigration on economic development, although these models suffer from a fundamental empirical weakness.[3] The major criticism of their concept of trapped economies centers on their hypothesis that an increase in income causes a rapid increase in population. Empirically the demographic changes necessary to continue this trap each year would be totally unrealistic. Thus, while popula-

[3] Professor Simon Kuznets questions the ability of population growth to exceed the growth of output for an extended period of time. That is, assuming that population and output are both growing at the rate of 2 per cent per year and the next year output growth reaches 3 per cent per year, it is almost impossible for population growth to jump from 2 per cent to 3 per cent within one year. It would require an abnormal demographic change that is not likely to be stimulated by a 1 per cent increase in output growth. Even if this phenomenal increase occurred, the next period of output growth to 4 per cent per annum would require a jump in population from 30 per thousand to 40 per thousand — one even more unlikely than the first. Short of unusual conditions, such as floods and epidemics, these magnitudes of demographic changes are unrealistic. The conclusion is that, although an economy can be stagnating and have population growth exceeding output growth, it is not in a strong trap. Harvard University, Seminar in Population and Economic Development, Spring 1964.

tion growth may initially exceed the growth of output causing stagnation and declining per capita incomes, the tenacity of the trap is overrated and can be broken with successive yearly attempts to raise output. Although it need not result in a strong trap, rapid population growth can prevent rapid increases in per capita income. The concept of a trap is employed for heuristic purposes, and it is important to note that it is not crucial for analysis of the effects of emigration on economic growth. The major goal of the development process is to raise the level of per capita income, and any activity which stimulates its rate of growth will be desirable. Thus, if emigration can cause an increase in the rate of growth of output while simultaneously reducing the rate of growth of population, the divergence between the two growth rates will lead to a more rapid increase in per capita income growth.

This version of the low-level income trap is not confined (as is Nelson's) to the short run, but operates over a longer time period until the stage of self-sustained growth is reached. Population growth is determined over the long period by changes in both death and birth rates. The rate of growth of output is determined by net capital formation, but the only source of capital is from increased savings. The initial assumptions of this study are that all land (which Nelson treats as additions to capital) is fully utilized and that increases in the supply of labor do not lead to increases in output because of a redundancy of labor; that is, the marginal product is zero in the case of disguised unemployment.

Major Hypotheses

Three basic hypotheses or equations determine the growth of output, population, and net capital formation. Output is a function of capital:

$$Y = f(K) \qquad (2.1)$$

where Y = output, K = capital. The model assumes that all savings are converted into productive capital. Foreign capital is exogenously determined. This gives an identity equation:

$$S = \triangle K \qquad (2.2)$$

where S = savings. Substituting the identity established in Equation 2.2, we get income as a function of savings:

$$Y = f(S). \qquad (2.3)$$

This second hypothesis asserts that savings per capita is a function of income per capita. The positive relationship between these two variables occurs after a certain minimum income per capita level is reached. Below this level of income per capita, either a zero or negative savings per capita will prevail; that is, total income will be spent on purchases of the necessities of life:

$$d(S/P) = g(d(Y/P)) \qquad (2.4)$$

is a positive function at (Y/P'), where $d(S/P) = $ change in savings per capita. Thus net capital formation is determined by the changes in per capita income.

Since the rate of growth of output is a function of the change in capital formation, then:

$$d(Y/Y) = h(d(S/P)) \qquad (2.5)$$

where $dY/Y = $ the rate of growth of output (income). Since the change in savings per capita is a function of changes in income per capita and the rate of growth of output is a function of the change in savings per capita, then by substituting the left-hand side of Equation 2.4 in Equation 2.5, we get the rate of growth of output as a function of income per capita; that is:

$$d(Y/Y) = h(d(Y/P)) \qquad (2.6)$$

It is assumed that as income per capita increases, savings per capita will increase at a decreasing rate approaching a constant proportion of income per capita at higher levels of per capita income. Thus the change in the rate of savings per capita will decrease and the marginal productivity of capital will fall as more capital is invested, causing a decline in the rate of growth of output at higher levels of per capita income. The curve reflecting the growth of output would exhibit decreasing returns or, in other words, a decelerated rate of growth. (The foregoing representation of the growth of output is similar to the Nelson model.)[4]

Population growth is defined in the traditional manner of crude births minus crude deaths and net emigration:

$$d(P) = B - D - M \qquad (2.7)$$

where $d(P) = $ change of population, $B = $ births, $D = $ deaths, and $M = $ net emigration. It is hypothesized that the birth rate is an

[4] Nelson, *op. cit.*

inverse function of income per capita after a certain high-level income per capita threshold is attained. Prior to reaching this threshold, the birth rate rises slightly in response to increased incomes and is nearly at the biological maximum.[5] The decline in the birth rate occurs at higher income levels because changes in the economic and social structure of the society influence the values and goals of the population and raise the cost of rearing children. Specifically, changes in attitudes and knowledge regarding family size and the ability to purchase contraceptive devices are the basic causes for a decline in birth rates at high income per capita levels. Symbolically,

$$d(B) = f(Y/P) \qquad\qquad (2.8)$$

The death rate is also an inverse function of income per capita but at lower levels of income. In recent times, this earlier decline of the death rate is usually not attributed to the level of income prevailing in the country but to large-scale government expenditures in the area of public health and preventive medicine. Nevertheless, these expenditures occur when the country has a low-level income and are the cause of rapidly falling death rates in very short periods of time. Despite the exogenous influence of government expenditures on the death rate, it is still considered to be a function of levels of income per capita:

$$d(D) = g(Y/P) \qquad\qquad (2.9)$$

The smaller the expenditure by the government in the area of public health, the more important the income per capita level is in determining the death rate changes. Lower incomes reflect poor sanitation, inadequate nutrition, and absence of medical facilities.

Now, if we assume that net emigration is zero, the rapid decrease in the death rate and the slowly increasing birth rate will cause a rapid growth of population at low levels of income per capita. Since the birth and death rates are both functions of income per capita, then, given the identity of Equation 2.7, the growth of population will also be a function of income per capita:

$$d(P/P) = h(Y/P) \qquad\qquad (2.10)$$

The time lag between the falling death and birth rates and the rate of change will determine the extent of the increases in popu-

---

[5] Leibenstein, *op. cit.*, discusses the concept of a biological maximum birth rate (3.5 per cent).

lation during the development period. Since death rates predominantly determine the rate of population growth at low levels of income per capita (after government expenditures in public health), rapid population growth will prevent the translation of gains in output growth into gains in the rate of growth of per capita income. In short, a low-level income in a stagnating economy can result from rapid increases in population that exceed or equal the increases in output. In some cases they cause an actual decline in per capita incomes.

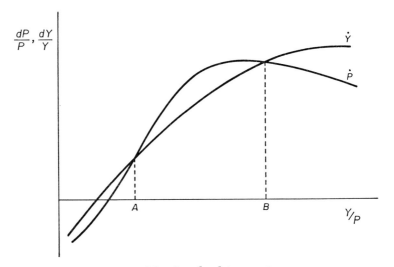

FIGURE 2.1.   *Low-level income trap.*

Figure 2.1 illustrates the typical low-level income trap. The rate of growth of output and population are both functions of income per capita. The slopes of the two curves at the point of intersection will determine the level of income per capita that results in a stable equilibrium position. Population growth is stimulated by both the growth of income per capita and large-scale government expenditures and accelerates to the point where it exceeds the rate of growth of income. The intersection of the two curves at a low level per capita income results in a stable equilibrium — Point A in Figure 2.1. The slope of the population growth curve is greater than the slope of the growth-of-output curve to the right of the intersection, forcing the income per capita to decrease to the level prevailing at Point A. To the left of Point A, the slope of the output curve is greater than the slope of the population curve and income per capita increases to Point A. Thus, any movement to the left or right of Point A sets in motion forces bringing income per capita to settle at Point A, the stable low-level equilibrium. (This figure is similar to Nelson's.)[6]

In Figure 2.1 the intersection of the output and population growth curves at Point B represents another critical stage of the economy's development. To the left of Point B, the growth of output exceeds the growth of population, and the economy experiences continuous increases in per capita income. This represents the stage of cumulative self-sustained economic growth. Point B is an unstable equilibrium, for any movement to the right will result in further increases in per capita income and any movement to the left will result in decreases until Point A, the stable equilibrium, is reached.[7] The size of the gap between stagnation and growth, Points A and B, respectively, is clearly a function of the shape of the two curves. In most underdeveloped countries population growth is increasing very rapidly and output growth is usually growing very slowly because of the scarcity of adequate capital formation. Thus the distance between the low-level income stagnation point and cumulative growth is often quite large and difficult to overcome.

Determinants of Population Growth

This population growth problem is similar to the case presented by Malthus;[8] the essential difference is the cause of the rapid increase in population. Malthus contended that rapid increases in the birth rate in response to rising incomes would cause the income per capita to fall back to its original subsistence level. Malthus' proposition is less plausible today, given the existence of extremely high birth rates and the vast reservoir of medical knowledge which can reduce death rates substantially in a very short period of time.

It is of considerable consequence whether the cause of the growth of population stems from a falling death rate or from an increase in the birth rate. The fall in the death rate due to public health

---

[6] Nelson, op. cit. Figure 11 is almost the same as Nelson's with the basic differences in the level of the trap and the timing of the decline in the growth of population.

[7] A similar trap concept is employed in the Solow model with reference to stable or increasing capital-labor ratios instead of the per capita income in the diagrams. Solow, op. cit.

[8] Kenneth Smith, The Malthusian Controversy (London: Routledge and Kegan Paul, 1951), pp. 5–6.

expenditures causes a more rapid increase in population than an increase in an already high birth rate. The result of a death-rate-determined population growth is a lower level of income per capita trap and a larger gap between equilibrium income and the point of cumulative economic growth, represented by Points *A* and *B*, respectively, in Figure 2.2. This Figure reveals the shape of the

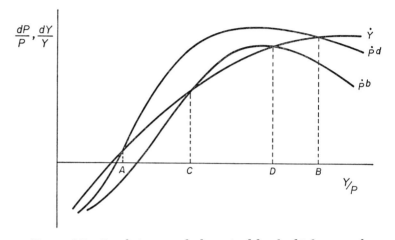

FIGURE 2.2.   *Population growth determined by the birth rate and population growth determined by the death rate.*

two different population curves — one determined predominantly by the decline in the death rate, labeled p^d, and the other by the rise in the birth rate, labeled p^b. The intersection of the p^d and Y curves reveals the low-level income trap at Point *A* and the cumulative income per capita level at Point *B*. The gap between the two points of per capita income is quite large and difficult to overcome. In contrast, the slower population growth curve p^b intersects the output curve Y at a significantly higher income per capita, representing a stable equilibrium at a much higher level.

In addition, because birth rates are already near the biological maximum, the rate of change of the birth rate in a downward direction emerges earlier and at a lower per capita income. This results in a lower intersection between the two curves and reduces the gap between a stable equilibrium and cumulative growth per capita income levels, represented by Points *C* and *D*, respectively. The more rapid rate of population growth resulting from rapid decreases in the death rate and modest increases in the birth rate seems to describe more accurately the prevailing population trends in many of the underdeveloped nations of the world. This rapid increase in the population growth, even if income traps are unrealistic and do not prevail empirically, creates a great obstacle to the goal of maximizing the rate of growth of income per capita in these countries.

Mechanisms to Stimulate Economic Development

What possible alternatives exist for solving the dilemma of a low-level income trap or for increasing the rate of growth of per capita income? Before proceeding to analyze two alternatives, it is necessary to examine why domestic measures cannot break the low-level income trap. The economy is severely hampered in stimulating the growth of output and in controlling the growth of population. The existence of low levels of income prevents the economy from generating sufficient amounts of savings for investment in productive enterprises. It is thus difficult to overcome the vicious circle in which low levels of savings prevent the growth of income without which additional savings are impossible.[9]

In controlling population growth, the government's power and influence are confined to limiting the birth rate. The decision to reduce the death rate by large expenditures for public health is not a rational economic calculation. It is based purely on political and humanitarian goals and is therefore not subject to manipulation merely for the successful achievement of economic goals. On the other hand, the birth rate is an elusive and difficult variable to control. The successful development of the country, bringing higher income and education levels, may be the most effective way

---

[9] The vicious circle of low income and low savings was proposed by Ragnar Nurkse, *Problems of Capital Formation in Underdeveloped Countries* (Oxford: Oxford University Press, 1953). This savings cycle has been criticized by Everett Hagen in a series of lectures delivered at M.I.T. Hagen stresses that many societies can increase their savings if the proper attitudes or propensities exist. It is not a problem of low income as much as a problem of attitudes and values of the traditional population. He points out that in many of these underdeveloped countries the income distribution is very unequal. The wealthier segment of the population can save significant amounts rather than consume expensive luxury items, if they so desire. Even the poor segment of the population can save, since very few are really living on the margin of subsistence. He cites the example of primitive societies being able to save for ritual ceremonies. This analysis also weakens the strength of a Nelson low-level income trap argument.

of influencing the birth rate. But a long period of growth is required before the gains of income, urbanization, and education
can permeate the values, attitudes, and actions of the population.
Thus, another vicious circle emerges: economic growth can control
population growth; but at low levels of income, population growth
prevents the desired economic growth from occurring. The international movement of two factors of production—labor outflow[10]
and capital inflow — offers a potential solution to this dilemma.

Injections of Foreign Capital

The injection of foreign capital resulting in increases in the
growth of output until it exceeds the growth of population is illustrated in Figure 2.3. The figure assumes that the capital output

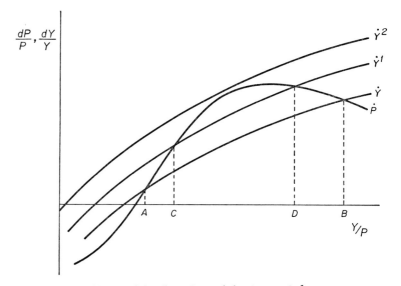

FIGURE 2.3.   *Injections of foreign capital.*

ratio is constant and that all foreign capital is invested in productive enterprises. A falling marginal productivity of capital is implicitly assumed by the shape of the output curve. The intersection
of the curves labeled P (population) and Y (output) illustrates
the same low-level income trap at Point A and cumulative growth

[10] United Nations, Department of Social Affairs, Population Division, *The
Determinants and Consequences of Population Trends,* Population Study No.
17 (New York: United Nations, 1953).

at Point B. Injections of foreign capital are represented by increases of output in curves labeled Y^1 and Y^2. Each larger amount of foreign capital lowers the gap between stagnation and growth, represented by the $C-D$ gap compared to the original gap of $A-B$. A very substantial increase in foreign capital (depending on the rate of population growth) enables the low-level income trap to be broken and output growth to exceed the growth of population at all levels of per capita income.

Large injections of capital can stimulate the growth of output so that it increases faster than the growth of population, but an important question is whether the quantity of capital required annually to reach this level of output growth could realistically be supplied. At the initial stages of economic development the capital-output ratio is usually higher than at later stages because of the large amounts of capital allocated to social overhead projects.[11] Let us assume for the purposes of an arithmetical illustration that the capital-output ratio at this initial stage is five. Thus, in order to achieve any increase in income per capita, capital formation must be at least five times more than the rate of increase in population. A country with rapid population growth of 3 per cent per annum would require a minimum of 15 per cent savings (investment of GNP) merely to maintain per capita income. A modest gain of 1 per cent in per capita income would require a rate of investment of 18 per cent of GNP. It is often beyond the ability of many developed economies to give, lend, or invest adequate amounts of capital.

Labor Emigration

The possible beneficial effects of labor emigration on an overpopulated economy are illustrated in Figure 2.4 The same conditions of a low-level income trap and cumulative growth are identified at Points A and B, respectively, but with the introduction of a migration hypothesis, several new population curves can be presented. Migration is considered to be a function of the differentials in income per capita between two countries:

$$d(M) = k(Y/P^a - Y/P^b) \text{ at } Y/P^3 \qquad (2.11)$$

where $dM =$ the change of emigration, $Y/P =$ income per capita,

[11] Paul N. Rosenstein-Rodan, "Notes on the Theory of the Big Push," unpublished paper, Massachusetts Institute of Technology, Center for International Studies, Cambridge, Massachusetts, March 1957.

subscripts a and b represent two different countries. Migration will not occur until a certain minimum income per capita (Y/P^3) is attained in the underdeveloped country. (This concept of minimum per capita income is discussed in more detail later in this chapter.) The greater the differential in income per capita levels, the larger the migration stream. As the differential narrows, the

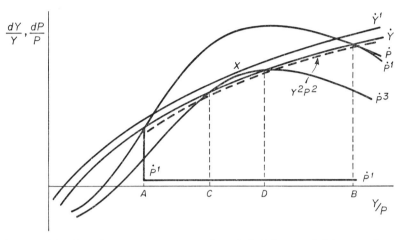

FIGURE 2.4.   *Simultaneous movement of capital inflow and labor outflow.*

migration stream will taper off and eventually cease when the income per capita in both countries approaches equality. The selection of per capita incomes as the key variables instead of wage rates was made because the former includes the employment conditions in the two regions.

One possibility is that the rate of migration equals the rate of natural increase (rate of births minus deaths) so that when the migration stream commences at Point A in Figure 2.4, the population curve is reduced to a zero rate of growth; that is, it runs along the horizontal axis from Point A to Point B. Under this assumption of the migration rate, migration eliminates all increases in population growth and, given the existing growth of output, it allows rapid and continuous growth of per capita income. The rate of growth of capital accumulation will now determine the rate of growth of income per capita. At the income per capita level of Point B, the differentials between the two countries are eliminated and migration ceases. Population growth resumes its curve, which at this level of income per capita is not so steep because a falling birth rate exceeds a slightly decreasing death rate. Higher levels of per capita income result in higher savings, stimulating the growth of output, while the declining population growth rate contributes to the continuous growth of income per capita.

The migration rate can be assumed to be of a magnitude that reduces the rate of natural increase to a level equal to the rate of growth of output. This is described by the curve labeled Y^2P^2, the identical rate of growth of output and population. Although it represents a stable income per capita at Point A, it provides favorable conditions to future growth of per capita income. Under these conditions, any increase in the rate of capital formation internally or externally will lead to increases in per capita income. Thus, if emigration alone is to stimulate the growth of per capita income, it must be great enough to reduce the rate of population growth below the growth of output each year.

Even if the migration rate does not reduce the population rate below the output growth rate, such as depicted by the curve labeled P^3, it does reduce the gap from the original points A and B to the new points C, the stable income, and D, the growth income.

It is possible to assume a rate of migration that can cause increases in income per capita without increases in capital accumulation — that is, a rate of migration sufficiently large to exceed the rate of natural increase, thereby causing actual reductions in the absolute number of the population. If this increase in income per capita stimulates greater rates of savings and, hence, raises total savings and capital formation, the economy may continue to experience increases in per capita income with a future reduction in the size of emigration.

On the basis of migration's effect on population alone, one can conclude that emigration that effectively reduces the growth of population during the initial phases of economic development can serve as a beneficial factor, stimulating the rate of growth of per capita income. The effect of emigration on both the growth of output and population simultaneously is examined later in this chapter.

Simultaneous Movements of the Factors of Production

On practical grounds, the ability of either factor of production — capital inflow or labor outflow — to overcome the population growth problem is questionable. The magnitude of the capital needed from abroad has been previously discussed. The size of effective migration from many of the larger countries often would also involve unrealistic movements of people. For illustrative purposes, a country with a population of 200 million and a 3 per cent growth of population would require a movement of 6 million people each year to reduce the growth of population to zero. Although the movement of either one of the factors alone may be unrealistic, the movement of both factors simultaneously would reduce the necessary magnitudes to a more reasonable level and speed up the rate of growth of per capita income to the level of self-sustained economic growth without either factor's mobility being crucial to the continuation of the growth of the economy.

The interaction of the movement of both factors of production is depicted in Figure 2.4. Limited migration has resulted in a growth of population labeled P^3 with a trap occurring at Point A. Combining limited migration with an injection of outside capital results in an increased growth of output depicted by the curve Y^1. The point of tangency between the two curves is an unstable equilibrium Point X because any movement to the right or left will set in motion forces causing output to grow faster than population (the slope of the output curve at all points to the right and left of X is greater than the slope of the population curve). Thus, a combination of reduced flows of capital and labor resulted in the elimination of the low-level income trap and stimulated the continuous growth of income per capita.

The timing and magnitude of emigration will determine how much capital is needed to overcome the stagnation, and conversely the size and timing of capital inflow will determine how much emigration is needed to reach a stage of cumulative economic growth. The ratio of labor outflow to capital inflow needed to raise income per capita will be identical to the capital-output ratio existing in the economy. Thus, a capital-output ratio of three will result in a substitution ratio of the factors of three. In other words, a rate of migration of 1 per cent is equivalent to a rate of capital investment of 3 per cent as far as its effect on raising income per capita is concerned.[12] (This has assumed implicitly that migration

---

[12] This substitution of capital and labor with respect to raising per capita income does not imply that the two factors are indeed perfect substitutes. The desirable effect of increased capital formation is preferable to the decrease of population. The additional capital inflow may be sufficient to employ many of these unemployed unproductive workers. Even if this were not the case, a country has an investment in its workers. Their departure from the country is a definite loss, while an inflow of capital does not cost the economy anything. Nevertheless, even though emigration would mean a loss of past investment,

does not affect output.) With capital scarce and labor redundant, any combination of the movements of the factors in the desirable directions will result in a reduction in the rate of growth of population and an increase in the rate of growth of output, stimulating the rate of growth of income per capita.

Independence of Economic and Demographic Variables

The basic model, presented above, assumed that the economic variables significantly influence the demographic variables during the development process. Specifically, it assumes that the birth rate is an inverse function of per capita income levels at higher incomes. Figure 2.5 describes the problem that emerges when

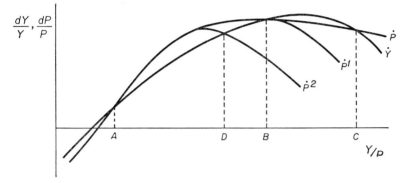

FIGURE 2.5.   *Interaction of economic and demographic growth.*

economic and demographic variables are independent. The rate of growth of output begins to decrease at high levels of income per capita, while population increases at a constantly high rate. This results in three intersections of the two curves at Points A, B, and C. Points A and C represent stable equilibrium points, while B is an unstable point. Despite rapid increases in output leading to growth of income per capita, the economy reaches a new point of stagnation at a high level of income. Since income per capita does not reduce the birth rate, the rate of population growth does not decrease as per capita income increases. The same problem would

---

if the workers remained unemployed the society would be investing even more scarce resources in them. Thus, capital inflow is more desirable, but it is also more difficult to obtain. Without enough capital inflow to employ the redundant laborers, emigration will prove to be beneficial for the society.

arise, even if we assumed that income growth does not decline when an exogenous increase in population occurs due to increased fertility, decreased deaths, or large-scale immigration. Thus, the greater the influence that economic variables have on demographic trends, the more desirable are continuous increases in per capita income during the crucial stages of economic development.

The level of income per capita necessary to initiate the inverse relationship between birth rates and per capita income is crucial to the determination of the point at which the population curve will fall below the growth of the output curve. Obviously, the greater the impact of rising income per capita and its concomitant educational, attitudinal, and behavioral changes on the birth rate, the shorter the lag between the fall in death and birth rates and the greater the gains in income per capita. Migration may not only reduce the population growth rate immediately but it may operate to reduce future birth rates at a lower income per capita level than would have been the case without migration. This phenomenon would depend on the characteristics of the migrants; if the younger and more reproductive members of the society emigrate, then a fall in the birth rate (at a lower income level) will occur, reducing the time lag between the falling death and birth rates. The differences in the timing of the fall in the birth rate are illustrated by the two population curves labeled P^1 and P^2 in Figure 2.5. The curve P^1 reflects a longer time lag between the fall in death and birth rates and intersects the output curve Y at a higher income per capita, Point B. Curve P^2, reflecting a shorter time lag, narrows the gap and cumulative growth occurs at a lower income per capita, Point D. With the population growth curve declining due to migration and the falling birth rate, a high-level income trap, depicted by Point C, is avoided and cumulative growth occurs. The same reasoning applies to the effect of emigration, whether or not a trap occurs. The only difference is that emigration increases the rate of growth of income per capita by reducing the population growth instead of enabling the economy to break the low-level income trap.

A Modification of the Theoretical Framework

A more realistic model requires certain basic modifications of the preceding hypotheses, even though establishing the validity of more complex propositions is costly and difficult.

The Migration Hypothesis

Up to this point the effects of emigration on the growth of output have been ignored. Whether emigration will stimulate the growth of output will depend on two factors: (*a*) the economic conditions at the time of emigration, and (*b*) the characteristics of the migrants. The economic conditions applicable to this analysis were stated earlier; and the most important for our purposes was the existence of unemployment, open and disguised. The original hypothesis, that migration was a function of the differentials in income per capita levels between two countries, does not provide any information on the characteristics of the migrants. The crucial impact of these characteristics on the rate of growth of output necessitates a modification of the hypothesis, which determines not only the direction of the migration but one that also provides an explanation of the characteristics of the migrants.[13] The characteristics of the migrants with respect to geographical origin, industry attachment, employment experience, savings and savings propensity, occupation, age and sex, education — all will exert significant influences on the rate of growth of output. The emigration of educated, skilled, employed workers with high propensities to save and large amounts of capital assets from a country experiencing a shortage of skilled labor and capital would have a serious negative effect on the rate of growth of output. On the other hand, the movement of unskilled, unemployed, uneducated, nonsaving, agricultural workers with limited capital assets would have a beneficial effect on the rate of growth of output.

The modified migration hypothesis states that migration is a function of two sets of differentials in per capita income: (*a*) absolute differentials in per capita income for each skill level or occupation, and (*b*) relative differentials of skilled to unskilled income per capita between two countries. Symbolically:

$$dM = f(Y/P_a{}^s - Y/P_b{}^s;\ Y/P_a{}^u - Y/P_b{}^u) \quad \text{at } Y/P^x \quad (2.11a)$$

$$dM = g\,\frac{Y/P^s}{Y/P^u} - \frac{Y/P^s}{Y/P^u} \qquad\qquad \text{at } Y/P^x \quad (2.11b)$$
$$\quad\ (a)\qquad\ (b)$$

---

[13] The migration hypothesis does not attempt to explain the variations in annual migration which will most likely be affected by employment conditions in the two countries. The combination of reduced costs and better knowledge does indicate that the migration stream should accelerate at a rapid rate

where $Y/P =$ income per capita, $Y/P^x =$ minimum income per capita necessary before emigration occurs, $s =$ skilled, $u =$ unskilled, a and $b =$ two different countries, $dM =$ change in migration. Part a of the hypothesis assumes that workers respond to income differentials that are relevant to their skill level or occupation. Part b reflects the basic pull factors of greater economic earning power in another area. On the other hand, it is hypothesized that people often consider in their decision to move the relative improvements in their economic position as a result of migrating. In short, those with the greatest incentive to migrate will be those who have the greatest absolute differential and can also improve their relative economic position with respect to other workers in the economy. The relative income differentials reflect not only a pull phenomenon but include a basic push factor. That is, those workers who are relatively worse off with respect to other workers in the economy have a greater incentive to migrate in order to alleviate the relatively impoverished conditions that envelop their daily lives. This perceived poverty gives them a greater desire to migrate compared to the relatively comfortable status quo of the elite of the economic community.

In addition to dictating the skill composition of the migration stream, the migration hypothesis also informs us that the age of the migrants will be younger than the remaining labor force. The greatest incentive to emigrate will fall upon those who can maximize the present discounted value of the economic differential in earnings. Clearly, the younger members of the labor force have a greater earning period in which to obtain the maximum benefit from the differential and thus will constitute the bulk of the migration stream.

Per Capita Income Threshold

Clarification of the concept of a minimum per capita income as a prerequisite for large-scale emigration is necessary. The nature of the migration hypothesis requires that the people with the greatest incentive to migrate — namely, the unskilled — have an income sufficient to cover the costs of migration. Since these unskilled workers will have incomes lower than the prevailing per capita income, the income per capita necessary for the large-scale emi-

---

(assuming that the demand for labor is constant) after the initial wave of early migrants.

gration of these people would have to be higher than usual.[14] Even before the costs of migration are considered, the concept of a minimal income implies different attitudes and psychological propensities to emigrate. Below this minimal level of income the population will not be cognizant of existing alternatives of improving their depressed economic standard of living. Their information, knowledge, attitudes, activities, and ambitions are rigidily structured by the traditional society that pervades their lives. A change from the status quo is severely restricted. The ability and courage to make a monumental decision to emigrate is almost impossible in such a traditional environment. At higher income per capita levels, education is increased, communication and information are vastly improved, and the breakdown of traditional values and attitudes occurs with greater rapidity.

The level of income per capita necessary to stimulate emigration is a direct function of the costs of migration. The two most significant costs are the transportation to the country of destination and the length of time without employment. The latter cost is often minimized as the number of migrants already living in the new area increases. The older migrants supply improved information, aid in finding employment, food, and shelter during the initial days of emigration. The first group of migrants would have higher costs and would require a larger fund of savings to carry them through the initial period without income. If the demand for labor in the advanced economy is high, the cost of unemployment (the loss of income) is reduced substantially. The commencement of the migration of unskilled labor would coincide with favorable employment conditions in the developed economy combined with rising income per capita levels and a reduction of transport costs. If the latter cost is prohibitive in relation to income levels, then voluntary migration of a large segment of the population will not occur, despite the strong push and pull forces. Only active and decisive government action in the form of transportation subsidies would enable a significant amount of the population to emigrate.

[14] The concept of minimum income per capita is not useful when the income distribution is very unequal. Despite high income per capita levels, the majority of the population, especially the unskilled rural segment, would not have attained the minimum income level to initiate a large-scale emigration. Because of this, it is expected that the early migrants will possess greater skills, education, and income than the remaining population. As conditions improve for the unskilled, rural population, the migration stream will comprise a greater number of them.

(It is not clear that the benefits of this allocation of government expenditures is superior to other alternatives, that is, education and so on.)

The usefulness of emigration as a positive factor in stimulating economic development of overpopulated, backward economic countries is restricted by this minimal income per capita needed to initiate large-scale emigration. If stagnation occurs at a low subsistence level of income per capita, voluntary migration will not occur, despite extremely significant differences in per capita income levels between countries. Yet, if foreign capital is forthcoming to stimulate the growth of per capita income, the necessary level of income may be attained; emigration can then absorb the increases in population resulting from the rising incomes.

Who Migrates?

The basic question remains: How does this modified migration hypothesis inform us whether skilled or unskilled workers will emigrate? The answer depends on the differential earnings of different groups of workers in the developed and underdeveloped countries. Empirical data indicate that the ratio of skilled to unskilled earnings is considerably narrower in the more developed economies. Thus, the greatest absolute earnings differential in percentage terms prevails between the unskilled workers in the two areas. This naturally results in the unskilled having the greatest desire to emigrate because their relative economic position will also be improved considerably. Therefore, the migration stream should consist of predominantly unskilled workers, although it is expected that some skilled workers will migrate in response to the absolute differentials in earnings. The push factors operating on the skilled workers are negligible. In addition, the noneconomic benefits given to the skilled elite of the economy are often sufficient to compensate for the difference in absolute income and hence retard the movement of significant amounts of skilled workers. Factors such as social status, native country, language and culture, prestige, community leadership, family and friends, ownership of property, all operate to reduce the incentive of the elite to emigrate to a new, uncertain, and perhaps hostile environment. In short, the noneconomic costs of migrating are greater than the direct economic benefits.

In summary, the structure of the migration hypothesis stimulates the movement of the unskilled workers of the economy in significantly greater number than the migration of skilled labor. The greater absolute and relative differentials for the unskilled reflecting greater push and pull factors will stimulate a large proportion of these unskilled workers to emigrate. It is quite possible also that as the unskilled migrants and/or their children acquire new skills, occupations, and industrial work habits, they may respond to the relatively favorable economic position of the skill in their home country. The result would be a return migration of skilled personnel.

Emigration and the Growth of Output

What implications does the movement of unskilled workers have on the growth of output? First, most unskilled workers will be employed or at least attached to the agricultural sector of the economy. One of the preconditions of my model is the existence of disguised unemployment in the agricultural sector. The marginal productivity of these workers is zero. Under these conditions a withdrawal of the workers via emigration would eliminate the excess supply of labor, causing output, productivity, and per capita income to increase. The reduction of the endowment of labor in this sector would result in higher capital-labor ratios and higher land-labor ratios, and in turn would increase per capita incomes. The rise in incomes should stimulate the amount and rate of savings. With the changed factor endowments, the increased savings can be invested in capital machinery which should increase the output and productivity and hence income per capita even further. Thus, the elimination of the disguised unemployed laborers may stimulate the mechanism by which the agricultural sector is transformed from a backward, stagnating, and impoverished industry to a dynamic, growing, and productive sector of the economy. Since agricultural output comprises a large proportion of the total output of the economy at early stages of economic growth, the changes in output attributed to elimination of the disguised unemployed will contribute significantly to a rapidly accelerating growth of total output. This contrasts with the original assertion that output will grow but at a decreasing rate.

Emigration of unskilled workers also affects the capital-labor ratio and the ratio of skilled to unskilled labor in the industrial sector of the economy. Income per capita is, in part, a function of the capital-labor ratio and the ratio of skilled to unskilled labor in the economy. Any favorable increases in these ratios would increase income per capita, which in turn stimulates greater savings and a faster growth of output. If the proportion of unskilled to skilled labor in the migration stream (which the hypothesis predicts will be very high) is greater than the proportion in the labor force, then an increase in the skill composition of the labor force will occur. This improved quality of the labor force will result in increased productivity and hence stimulate increases in per capita income. The quality of the labor force will increase even more with the return flow of skilled labor and the additional educational opportunities made available by the departure of people who would have utilized the existing educational facilities.[15]

In addition, emigration of redundant workers should reduce government expenditures on welfare payments such as unemployment compensation, disability payments, and relief benefits. The reduction of government expenditures on welfare expenses and other social overhead investments such as education, sanitation, and health allows for the investment of additional capital funds in more productive projects. This should increase the amount of government investment contributing to increased growth of output.

The normal reduction of the capital-output ratio resulting from a decline in the amount of capital invested in social overhead projects also contributes to an accelerated rate of growth of output.

A Savings Hypothesis

The final change affecting the growth of output requires a modification of the savings hypothesis. The basic change is that savings

[15] Migration of a large segment of the younger members of the population increases the availability of limited educational facilities. The children and future children of the migrants are withdrawn from the country allowing the facilities and new allocations to education to be utilized by the remaining school-age population. The number of children allowed to use the facilities is increased, the teacher-pupil ratio and the quality of instruction is improved. An illustration would clarify the point.

Assume the economy allocates the sum of $1,000,000 to education per annum. The cost per child per annum is $200, the current enrollment is 40,000 children; next year an additional 14,000 students will be entering school. The school budget can afford only 10,000 new students. There will be 4,000 students deprived of an education, a situation that will probably be irreversible. Only if 4,000 children drop out of school will the system be able to accommodate the increased enrollment. Emigration of these children with their parents would alleviate the condition. It can prevent the deprivation of an education to people who are in desperate need of it. In this sense, future new entrants into the labor force will possess more education and greater skills. This gain must be balanced off by the loss to the society of children departing with their education. Clearly, the loss is reduced if the children return at a later age.

will increase, after a minimum per capita income level is attained, at an accelerated rate rather than at a decreasing rate; eventually it also approaches a constant proportion of income per capita. The rationale for proposing this modification is the reduction of the nonsaving population and the extremely precarious nature of the economic marketplace. The fluctuations and inefficiencies in the economy cause uncertainty in employment, earnings, and profits. This uncertainty stimulates the population (after a minimum income per capita is attained for basic consumption items) to save greater amounts out of their increased income. Thus, laborers experiencing high rates of unemployment, farmers experiencing fluctuating incomes, businessmen and entrepreneurs experiencing fluctuating profits, and peasants eager to save in order to acquire their own land — all will be motivated to increase their rate of savings to avoid the excessive hardships of an unstable fluctuating economy.[16] The result is an acceleration in the capital formation of the economy leading to an acceleration in the growth of output.

In summary, the migration of unskilled, rural, and unemployed workers will have a positive effect on the growth of output. Improved capital-labor ratios, reduced unemployment, increased savings, improved quality of the labor force, reduction of government expenditures on social overhead projects and welfare benefits, and lower capital-output ratios, higher land-labor ratios — all are results of emigration, either directly or indirectly. The total effect causes an accelerated rate of growth of output during the time of large-scale emigration. Thus, output growth increases rapidly, population growth decreases rapidly, and the rate of growth of income per capita is accelerated significantly.

The migration hypothesis asserts that the bulk of the migration stream will consist of young labor force members. The reduction of these reproductive members of the population will have a significant impact on the age structure of the population. The birth rate will decline as the size of the reproductive population is decreased. This will affect the growth of future generations of the population because a smaller birth rate will be reflected in a smaller reproductive population in the next generation. For our illustrative purposes, the emigration will cause an earlier decline

---

[16] Professor Milton Friedman proposed different consumption functions among various groups of people in the economy with the concept of permanent and transitory incomes. Milton Friedman, *A Theory of the Consumption Function* (Princeton, N.J.: Princeton University Press, 1957).

in the birth rate than normally expected, reducing population growth and increasing the rate of growth of per capita income.

Operation of the Model

Figure 2.6 illustrates the effect of migration on the growth of output and population. The figure reveals that emigration which affects only the population curve cannot stimulate the economy to

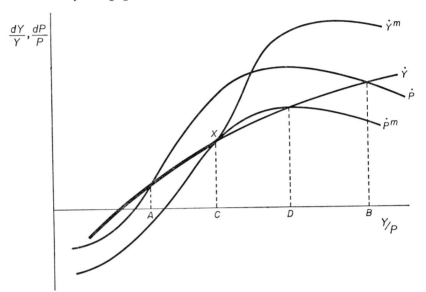

$$\frac{dY}{Y}, \frac{dP}{P}$$

$\dot{Y}^m$

$\dot{Y}$

$\dot{P}$

$\dot{P}^m$

X

A C D B

Y/P

FIGURE 2.6. *Effect of emigration on the growth of output and population.*

a level of income that will bring about self-sustained growth in per capita income. The orginal population curve reflects rapid growth in population, resulting from a sharply decreasing death rate B. The original output curve Y reflects a decreasing rate of growth. The intersection at Point A is again the low-level income trap and Point B the level of income leading to cumulative growth. The trap concept is used again as a heuristic device. The second population curve P^m reflects a slower rate of population growth because of emigration. Despite the reduction in population, the growth of population does accelerate as migration slows down and a new intersection occurs at Point C. A new income trap emerges at a higher level of income per capita. Point D reflects a lower level of income needed to reach a cumulative growth stage. Thus, migration has lowered the gap between the trap and growth stages, but has not broken the vicious circle of population growth outstripping output growth. Now, introducing the output curve labeled Y^m, reflecting an accelerated rate of growth of output due to emigration, the combined effects of emigration enable the economy to break the trap and experience continuous growth in per capita income. If a trap did not occur, the effect of emigration would have been similar, causing a more rapid rate of growth of per capita income than otherwise would have prevailed in the absence of emigration. The tangency of Y^m and P^m at Point X is unstable, and growth of income per capita occurs on either side of the tangency point. The accelerated stage of output growth coincided with the acceleration in population growth; but the former growth rate was significantly greater than the latter (after emigration), and income per capita increased.

In summary, the two basic differences from the final model and the earlier version occurred in the shape of the output and population growth rates. The modification of the migration hypothesis revealing the characteristics of the migrants caused an accelerated growth of output during the migration period and an earlier decrease in population growth. Emigration stimulated the rate of growth of output in the following ways: (a) agricultural output and productivity increased at an accelerated rate with the elimination of the disguised redundant workers; (b) savings per capita and total savings increased at an accelerated rate as per capita income rose; (c) the quality of the labor force increased as a result of the migration of unskilled workers and the increased education of the remaining labor force; (d) the capital-labor ratio increased, leading to increased output per worker; and (e) a reduction of government expenditures on social overhead projects, educational expenses, and welfare payments allowed the government to invest in productive projects.

The rate of growth of population was reduced directly by the migration stream itself and indirectly by a loss of reproductive members of the population. This latter reduction caused a drop in the birth rate, especially since rural persons, composing the bulk of the stream, had higher fertility rates. The total effect was an immediate reduction of the short-run population growth and fundamental demographic changes that would reduce the long-run population growth.

In short, the emigration stimulated a growing divergence between the two rates of growth, causing a very rapid rate of increase in the per capita income and the standard of living of the remaining population.

Emigration with Full Employment

What would the effect of continued emigration be when the excess supply of labor was reduced via emigration and the economy was operating under full employment of labor? With either an increased demand for labor and/or the reduction in the supply of labor, a labor shortage exists stimulating increases in real wage rates. The marginal productivity of capital will fall as real wages increase. If investment is a function of the marginal productivity of capital, this should reduce the rate of investment and cause a reduction in the future growth of the economy. The decrease in the rate of investment is avoidable if total productivity increases at a rate equal to or greater than the rise in real wages. The rate of return on capital under these conditions will not decrease. A rapid rate of productivity exceeding the rate of increase in wages can be accomplished by either public or private controls on wage rates. It would be more desirable if the newly invested capital contained significant amounts of technological change, causing very rapid increases in productivity. The reservoir of technical knowledge available to many of the underdeveloped countries gives them the opportunity to increase total productivity substantially in a short period of time with heavy investment in industries that possess recent vintage capital equipment.

Furthermore, if investment is a function of rates of return on alternative projects, then decreasing marginal productivity of capital may not retard investment as long as the returns remain higher than existing alternatives in other countries. This type of investment criterion gives the government's fiscal policies a direct role in stimulating further investment by reducing corporate profits taxes to a level where the net profits are clearly superior to existing alternatives. In either case, it is not clear that an increase in real wages will result in decreases in the rate of investment, thus retarding economic growth.

In addition, it is quite possible that increased real wages may stimulate demand for a variety of new goods previously not produced in the economy. With tariff protections for the infant industries, increased demand may stimulate increased investment.

The rising wages resulting from either increased demand or a reduced supply of labor may stimulate investment in capital-intensive industries with laborsaving machinery. This type of investment, of course, will not generate large amounts of employment, especially for unskilled jobs, and may cause a factor proportions problem[17] with a growing amount of unemployment among the unskilled laborers. If emigration absorbs the unemployed workers, the economy will probably grow at an even more rapid rate with the use of capital-intensive machinery and skilled labor resulting in significant increases in productivity.

"Effective" Migration Rates

The "effective" rate of emigration is determined, in part, by the economic objectives of the country. In my model, the objective was rapid increases in per capita income. This required a rate of migration that would reduce the rate of growth of natural population increase below the rate of growth of output.

If I decided instead that my objective would be to reduce or eliminate unemployment and maintain or increase the capital-labor ratio, a different rate of effective migration would emerge. A rising capital-labor ratio results in a rising output per laborer. However, it does not necessarily result in a rising income per capita. Only if the change in output per laborer is sufficiently large to offset the increase in dependent population will per capita income increase. Otherwise we will have a rising capital-labor ratio, rising output per worker, and decreasing per capita income. Now, if the labor force participation rate increased at a rate equivalent to the rate of increase of the population while the capital-labor ratio increased, then output per worker and also income per capita will increase. Thus a combination of increased output per worker and a higher labor force participation rate can counterbalance the growth of population and allow gains from the increased capital-labor ratio to be translated into gains in per capita income. If emigration reduces the labor force participation rate, then greater increases in the capital-labor ratio and productivity are needed to prevent per capita income from decreasing. Conversely, if the migrants were unemployed and classified as dependent, nonproductive workers and their emigration would reduce the dependency proportion, gains in per capita income would result.

[17] Richard S. Eckaus, "Factor Proportions in Underdeveloped Countries," *American Economic Review*, Vol. XLV (September 1955), pp. 539–565.

The achievement of a dual objective of a reduction of unemployment or avoidance of all unemployment (full employment) and a rising capital-labor ratio requires a different rate of effective migration. At first we assume that the labor force (labor supply L^s) is a constant proportion of the population. Unemployment is defined as the labor supply minus the demand for labor, that is, the residual of labor force minus employment. In order to achieve an increasing capital-labor ratio, it is necessary that the rate of growth of net capital investment, dK/K, be greater than the rate of growth of the demand for labor, dL^d/L^d.[18] Yet, in order to reduce existing unemployment, the rate of growth of the demand for labor will have to exceed the rate of growth of the supply of labor. Thus, dK/K must be greater than dL^d/L^d, which must be greater than d^sL^s/L^s. Now, we assume that the rate of growth of the demand for labor is a function of the rate of growth of net investment. If the economy is at the income per capita level where the rate of growth of population, dP/P, exceeds the rate of growth of output, dY/Y, then the supply of labor (constant proportion of population), dL^s/L^s, will be greater than the rate of growth of net investment, dK/K. The K/L^d ratio will increase, but the K/L^s will decrease. The result is growing unemployment, dL^u/L^u, with increases in the real wages of the employed workers. A growing imbalance in the distribution of income occurs with the skilled workers, working with more capital, increasing their income significantly. The smaller number of fortunate workers who are employed become wealthier while the growing number of unemployed workers live under impoverished subsistence incomes.

Under these conditions the rate of effective migration is one which absorbs the excess supply of labor (the rate of growth of the unemployed); thus dL^u/L^u. This rate allows the excess to be withdrawn without creating shortages of labor, stimulating a rise in wage rates at the expense of potential investment.

Dropping the restrictive and unrealistic assumption of constant proportionality between the labor force and population, we postulate that as the economy industrializes the labor force participation rate increases during the early stages of development. The increase results from a greater participation of women in the labor force as traditional values break down and women workers are accepted, lighter industrial and office work becomes available, and

---

[18] This statement implies that the investment of capital is basically labor-saving or capital-intensive.

there are fewer children to raise. The increased participation rate now requires a different rate of effective migration from the one needed to reduce the population growth below the growth of output. With the goals of reducing unemployment and raising capital-labor ratios, the effective rate of migration must be equal to or greater than the rate of change in unemployment, which is now growing faster than the population because of increased labor force participation. If disguised unemployment exists, the effective rate of emigration must be equal to the increase in unemployment plus some fraction of the existing amount of disguised unemployment.

Considering the unemployment and capital-labor ratio effects, an increasing ratio of labor force to population would normally require a larger number of migrants than if the labor force merely grew proportionally to population (assuming the demand for labor remained the same). Yet the migration stream should have a higher proportion of people in the labor force than the existing proportion within the country, and so the migration necessary to produce an effective result should be smaller than that necessary to reduce the growth of population below the growth of output.[19] This smaller migration stream, composed of a greater proportion of the labor force than in the economy, causes a reduction in unemployment and an increase in the capital-labor ratio in the economy.

Now, if the labor force participation rate of the migratory stream is identical to the rate in the economy, the same rate of migration would be necessary to achieve per capita increases and the prevention of increased unemployment. A higher rate would be necessary to increase the capital-labor ratio. If the labor force participation rate remains constant and is the same for the economy and the

[19] An illustration would clarify the differences in the effective rates of emigration. Fifteen years ago the population of the country was growing at 3 per cent, or 3,000 per year, with a population of 100,000. The labor force participation rate was 50 per cent; thus in the current year the new entrants into the labor force would total 1,500 (assuming that everyone enters at age fifteen). Assume also that there was no change in the demand for labor and net capital investment and the rate of growth of output is zero. Under these conditions a 3 per cent reduction of population, or 3,000 migrants per year are needed to maintain existing standards of income per capita. Now, if the reduction of unemployment is the objective, the size of the migration stream required is less, if the labor force participation rate of the migrants is greater than 50 per cent (the rate in the economy). If we assume that 70 per cent of the migrants are labor force members, then a migration stream of 2,200 will assure a reduction of the labor force, which is greater than the 1,500 new additions. The results are a reduction in the labor supply and a possible increase in the capital-labor ratio and output-labor ratio.

migration stream, there will be no difference in the effective rate of migration in order to achieve all three goals. A rising labor force participation rate would require a higher migration rate to accomplish the capital-labor ratio and unemployment goals. A higher labor force participation rate among the migrants would result in a smaller migration rate than the one needed to achieve the goal of increasing per capita income.

In summary, the effective rate of migration is a function of the demand for labor (determined by capital investment) and the labor supply (determined, in part, by the growth of population and the labor force participation rate). During the latter stages of economic growth, population growth should decline, labor force participation rates at first should rise and then fall, approaching a constant proportion of population, and the rate of growth of capital investment, a function of growing income per capita, should increase and then eventually decrease. Under these conditions, if labor supply decreases faster than capital formation, income per capita will continue to increase and the migration stream eventually will be eliminated as the differentials in income per capita are reduced. Even if the differential in income per capita does not decrease, the rising levels of income in the home country should reduce the incentive to emigrate. In short, the push factors would be eliminated.

Unsolved Problems

When does the effect of emigration on income per capita become negative? In static terms, the emigration of a worker who earns more than the average worker earnings (assuming that he emigrated with his family and did not affect the dependency proportion of the population) would cause a reduction in income per capita and income per worker. In semidynamic terms, emigration would exert a negative effect on income per capita when the reduction of output exceeded the reduction in population growth rates. But both of these formulations are subject to the same criticism of "optimum population" concepts. The concept is basically a static one, neglecting the effects of changes in tastes, technology, attitudes, and basic behavior of the remaining population.

On this basis it is difficult to discuss the effects on the economy when employed workers emigrate. If wage rates rise, does investment fall or does it merely stimulate the change in the type of capital investment from labor-using to laborsaving? If employed workers leave, does this stimulate, in later periods, an improved quality of the labor force? And how does one balance off the costs in dollar terms of rearing and educating the migrants, whether they be employed or unemployed? If the workers are unemployed, with little chance of becoming productive in the future, is it better to write off the cost of investment rather than to continue to support the unproductive population? Where would the unemployed be better off, both economically and socially? These are examples of the difficult nature of analyzing the effects of emigration on the economic growth of a country. The chapters that follow examine empirically the effects of Puerto Rican emigration on the growth of the island of Puerto Rico.

3

Emigration and Population Growth in Puerto Rico

Introduction: The Demographic Revolution

The theoretical framework presented in Chapter 2 described the potentially harmful effect of rapid population growth in underdeveloped, stagnating economies. The growing literature[1] on population problems contains an abundant amount of statistics citing the extraordinary growth of the world's population. For example: ". . . it took 200,000 years for the world's population to reach 2,500 million, it will not take a mere thirty years to add another 2,000 million."[2]

This population explosion is especially alarming because many of the underdeveloped countries have limited resources available to support their populations. The United Nations population survey reports:

> Despite the inadequacy of statistical data, it is evident that there has recently been a widespread acceleration of population growth in the underdeveloped countries. The reason for this tendency is clear:

[1] United Nations, Department of Social Affairs, Population Division, *The Determinants and Consequences of Population Trends*, Population Study No. 17 (New York: United Nations, 1953); Philip M. Hauser, ed., *The Population Dilemma* (Englewood Cliffs, N.J.: Prentice-Hall, 1963); Alfred Sauvy, *Fertility and Survival* (New York: Criterion Books, 1961); Fairfield Osborn, ed., *Our Crowded Planet* (London: George Allen and Unwin, 1962).

[2] United Nations, Department of Economic and Social Affairs, Population Division, *The Future Growth of the World Population*, Population Study No. 28 (New York: United Nations, 1958), p. v.

the decline in mortality is responsible for a widening gap between the birth and death rates.[3]

The existence of extremely high birth rates in many of these countries, accompanied by widespread use of public health activities and preventive medicine which have reduced the death rate significantly, has resulted in the rapidly growing population, commonly referred to as the "demographic revolution." This demographic phenomenon is described from a statistical perspective by Eugene Black:

> There are movements in the less developed countries which vitiate all efforts to raise world living standards. One of the most massive obstacles is the tremendous rise in the populations of already crowded countries. For every four persons on earth in 1950, there are today five; in forty years there will probably be ten. In the past half-minute alone, about ninety babies will have been born into the world; only sixty persons will have died, leaving a net increase of thirty, or one every second. This rate of growth last year added the equivalent of the population of Italy to the world's millions, and the rate seems to be accelerating. In 1962 it will probably push the population of the world past the three billion mark, and it will double that figure before the end of the century.[4]

The presentation of statistics revealing the alarming rate of population growth is not meaningful without some relative basis for comparison. The cries of "standing room only" are only relevant when they are compared to the ability of the world's economic structure, propelled by the rapid rate of technological progress, to provide improvements in the standard of living for the expanding population.[5] Density of population or the rate of growth of population does not indicate per se whether population growth will result in unfavorable economic conditions for the population. The density of population in the northeastern section of the United

[3] United Nations, Department of Social Affairs, Population Division, *The Determinants and Consequences of Population Trends*, Population Study No. 17 (New York: United Nations, 1953), p. 263.

[4] Eugene Black, "Population Increase and Economic Development" in Osborn, *op. cit.*, p. 67.

[5] Everett E. Hagen, "Population and Economic Growth," *American Economic Review*, Vol. XLIV, No. 3 (June 1959), pp. 310–327. In this article Professor Hagen stresses the importance of rapid technological progress as the key mechanism supporting additional increases in the future population. It is the growth of technological progress, not population growth, that is the most significant occurrence of the first half of the twentieth century.

States and in the northwestern section of Europe is among the world's highest; yet the standard of living in these two regions is also among the world's highest. A strong and growing economy can often provide adequate improvements in the standard of living, despite increased population growth and a high density of population.

Population Growth: A Serious Obstacle

It is primarily in the underdeveloped economic areas where it is questionable whether the economy can support an expanding population and still provide for growing per capita incomes. At present in many of these countries the economies cannot provide adequate incomes for the existing population. Rapid population growth in these areas presents an obstacle for future improvements in per capita incomes and in some cases threatens to reduce the meager subsistence incomes. The United Nations report states the problem clearly:

> The problem of economic development is to increase production at a rate in excess of the rate of population growth. The amount of the increase in production necessary to achieve this purpose is obviously greater in a country where the population is growing rapidly than it is in one where population growth is slower. With population growing at the rate recently observed in Ceylon and Puerto Rico, production must be doubled in less than three decades if per capita output is to rise.[6]

The United Nations report isolated the small island of Puerto Rico as an illustration of the serious problem that rapid population growth presents to successful economic growth. With the danger of rapid population growth in Puerto Rico, it will be useful to examine the population problem of Puerto Rico and the effect of large-scale emigration from the island to the mainland of the United States.

The theoretical discussion in Chapter 2 asserted that emigration was an endogenous activity in the economic growth process. Specifically, emigration will have a more favorable impact on the growth process by reducing the population growth in both the short and long run if the size of the migration stream is large in relation to the population growth and if the composition of the migration

---

[6] United Nations, Population Study No. 17, *op. cit.*, p. 263.

stream consists of a greater proportion of reproductive people than the proportion within the country. In contrast to the theoretical conclusion, the United Nations population survey concludes that there are many experts who disagree with the practical usefulness of emigration as a means of solving the population problem. In response to the report of the United Nations mission to Haiti, which recommended that serious consideration should be given to emigration as a means of relieving the acute population pressure, several objections were raised:

> First, it has been argued that emigration on a scale sufficiently large to materially affect the rate of population growth is very difficult or impossible to achieve. Second, it has been pointed out that even large-scale emigration would be ineffective in the long run, since it would not correct the causes of the demographic imbalance in the countries of emigration.[7]

The lack of consensus on the effects of emigration on population growth creates a need for additional empirical studies. Often the difficulty is a lack of countries with rapid population growth and also a significant amount of emigration. Fortunately, Puerto Rico experienced both phenomena during the 1940–1960 period. The major objective of this chapter is to examine the direct and indirect effects of emigration on the growth of the Puerto Rican population.

Preconditions in Puerto Rico

In 1940 the island of Puerto Rico, the smallest and most easterly of the islands of the Greater Antilles in the Caribbean Sea, was a typically backward, traditional agrarian economy. The economy was dependent on sugar and was a one-crop, export-oriented island with a small land area, a large and growing population and very low per capita incomes. At this time the population of the island was 1,869,255, with approximately 67 per cent of the population living in rural areas.[8] The total land area was 2,191,000 acres, and nearly 70 per cent of this land was hilly or mountainous.[9] The small land area and the large population gave rise to a population density of 546 persons per square mile—one of the highest in the

[7] *Ibid.*, p. 306.
[8] Harvey S. Perloff, *Puerto Rico's Economic Future* (Chicago, Ill.: University of Chicago Press, 1950), p. 50.
[9] *Ibid.*, p. 8.

world. The scarcity of fertile productive land resulted in even
higher labor to cultivable land ratios (2.2 per acre),[10] causing an
extremely low per capita income — $125 per year in 1940.[11] Under
these adverse conditions, rapid increases in the population, especially in the rural sector, would have had a significant impact on
the growth of per capita income.

Population Growth in Puerto Rico

Changes in Mortality Rates

Commencing in 1940, a fundamental demographic change occurred on the island of Puerto Rico, which operated simultaneously
for the benefit and to the detriment of the population. Significant
public health expenditures by the government, rising per capita
income levels, the introduction of preventive medicine, the eradi-
cation of malaria and other tropical diseases, improved sanitation
and nutrition — all contributed significantly to the sharp decrease
in the mortality rate. Prior to 1940, the death rate averaged approximately 20 per thousand. Table 3.1, column 3, describes the annual
changes in the death rate. The rapid decrease in the death rate occurred from 1940 with a rate of 18.4 to 1950 with a rate of 9.9 per
thousand. The death rate continued to fall throughout the decade
of the 1950's at a slower but significant rate, reaching an all-time
low of 6.7 per thousand in 1962. In a ten-year period, 1940–1950,
the death rate decreased by 46 per cent, and for the entire twenty-
two year period it decreased by 65 per cent. Additional reductions
in the death rate will no doubt come about even slower than the
past changes because the fund of medical knowledge has been fully
implemented and future discoveries in the medical field will be
more difficult to achieve.

During the period of time from 1940 to 1947 the birth rate, which
had averaged approximately 40 per thousand prior to 1940, began
to rise, reaching a peak of 43.2 per thousand in 1947. The growing
birth rate and declining death rate together resulted in a very rapid
rate of natural increase, rising from 20.1 per thousand in 1940 to
an all-time high of 31.2 per thousand in 1947. In other words, an
increase from a 2 per cent to a 3 per cent population growth occurred in a short seven-year interval. The demographic changes

[10] *Ibid.*, p. 47.
[11] *Ibid.*, p. 160.

TABLE 3.1

BASIC COMPONENTS OF PUERTO RICAN POPULATION GROWTH

(*All rates are per thousand population*)

Year	Birth Rate	Death Rate	Rate of Natural Increase	Net Migration Rate	Rate of Population Increase
1940	38.5	18.4	20.1	0.2	19.9
1941	39.8	18.6	21.2	0.3	20.1
1942	40.3	16.6	23.7	0.7	23.0
1943	39.6	14.7	24.9	1.6	23.3
1944	41.0	14.8	26.2	5.5	20.7
1945	42.3	14.1	28.1	6.6	21.5
1946	42.6	13.2	29.4	19.2	10.8
1947	43.2	12.0	31.2	11.1	20.1
1948	40.8	12.2	28.6	15.2	13.4
1949	39.2	10.7	28.5	11.3	17.2
1950	38.5	9.9	28.6	15.2	13.4
1951	37.8	10.1	27.7	23.8	3.9
1952	36.4	9.3	27.1	26.1	1.0
1953	35.5	8.2	27.3	31.7	—4.4
1954	35.5	7.7	27.8	9.8	18.0
1955	35.4	7.3	28.1	20.4	7.7
1956	34.9	7.4	27.5	23.4	4.1
1957	33.8	7.1	26.7	16.9	9.8
1958	33.2	7.0	26.2	12.1	14.1
1959	32.3	6.8	25.5	12.9	12.6
1960	32.2	6.7	25.5	6.9	18.6
1961	31.4	6.8	24.6	0.7	23.9
1962	30.9	6.7	24.2	4.4	19.8

Source: Data of birth and death rates from Commonwealth of Puerto Rico, Department of Health, Division of Demographic Registry and Vital Statistics, *Annual Vital Statistics Report* (San Juan, Commonwealth of Puerto Rico, 1962), p. 2.

pushed Puerto Rico into an explosive population growth category — over 3 per cent per annum. This increase was equivalent to a 50 per cent increase in the growth rate of the population. Professor Perloff, viewing the alarming rate of population growth in Puerto Rico, wrote in 1948:

The basic population trends in Puerto Rico point to the inescapable fact that, in the absence of a thoroughgoing policy of population control, the population of the island will expand during the next generation at a very rapid rate.[12]

[12] *Ibid.*, p. 208.

Population change is usually defined as births minus deaths minus net emigration. Eliminating emigration results in a purely demographic determination of population growth, termed the rate of natural increase. The rate of natural increase and the rate of population increase were almost identical prior to 1940, due to negligible amounts of net emigration. The average net emigration for years prior to 1940 was approximately 2,400 per year, although considerable fluctuation occurred. (Appendix A presents the amount of migration from 1910 to 1962.) The rate of population increase by census years is presented in Table 3.2. Although the rate of popu-

TABLE 3.2

POPULATION OF PUERTO RICO AND THE ANNUAL RATE OF POPULATION
INCREASE FOR THE CENSUS YEARS 1899–1960

Year	Population	Annual Rate of Increase (per cent)
1899	953,243	
1910	1,118,012	1.5
1920	1,299,809	1.6
1930	1,543,013	1.7
1940	1,869,255	1.9
1950	2,210,703	1.7
1960	2,349,544	0.6

Source: United States Department of Commerce, Bureau of the Census, *United States Census of Population: 1960,* Final Report PC(11-53 A) (Washington, D. C., United States Government Printing Office, 1961), Table 1.

lation increase rose slightly for the first forty years, 1900–1940, it did not present a very serious problem, averaging approximately 1.7 per cent per annum. Comparing the rate of natural increase from 1940 to 1947 (see Table 3.1, column 4) with the moderate rate of 1.7 per cent prior to 1940, it is easy to observe the severe population growth problem that emerged on the island during the 1940's.

The Effects of Puerto Rican Emigration on Population Growth

Professor Perloff, writing in 1948, commented on the potential role of emigration in reducing the growth of population:

> Only since the end of World War II has emigration from Puerto Rico reached sizable proportions. There is no assurance, however, that the current movement will be sustained for any length of time or

that it will relieve the pressure of population within the next few generations.[13]

The theoretical discussion asserted that the migration stream would have continued until per capita income levels of the two regions were equated, which would require, under reasonable circumstances, a long period of time. In addition, the migration stream would be composed of reproductive members of the population which would affect the future birth rates and fertility patterns of the remaining population. Did the Puerto Rican emigration experience conform to the theoretical expectations?

The Magnitude of the Migration

During a short time span of fifteen years, 1945–1960, two interrelated and fundamental changes occurred which prevented the rapid rate of natural increase from being translated into rapid population growth. The most significant event was the commencement of the large-scale emigration of Puerto Ricans to the United States in 1945. Prior to 1945 the amount of Puerto Rican emigration was extremely small and had very little impact on the growth of population. The number of migrants during the period 1910 to 1945 was 91,000, or approximately 2,600 per year. Appendix A reveals that 45 per cent of the migration prior to 1945 occurred during the decade of the 1920's, when 42,000 people emigrated. A structural change in the size and rate of migration occurred at the end of the Second World War. From 1945 to 1962 nearly 578,000 Puerto Ricans emigrated to the United States; this constituted 85 per cent of the total emigration during the twentieth century. The largest number of people (446,800) emigrated during the period 1950–1960, comprising 65.6 per cent of the total emigration.

The rate of net migration per thousand people in the Puerto Rican population is presented in Table 3.1, column 5, for the years 1940–1962. The size and rate of net migration was of sufficient magnitude to effectively reduce the actual population growth. Figure 3.1 illustrates pictorially the rate of births, deaths, and migration per thousand people for the period 1910–1962. Migration began to play a significant role in the demographic changes in the island in 1940, and in 1945 it became the dominant factor (it was greater than the death rate) in reducing the population growth. It remained the dominant factor throughout the fifteen-year period,

---

[13] *Ibid.*, p. 205.

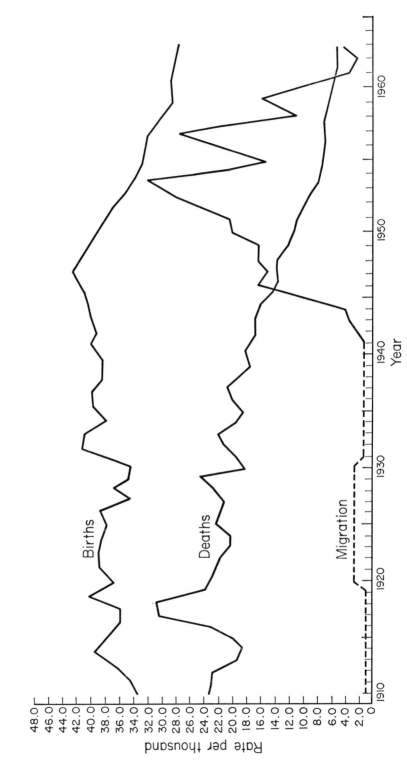

FIGURE 3.1. *Birth, death, and migration rates in Puerto Rico 1910–1963.*

until 1962 when the migration rate dropped below the death rate.

The rate of net migration increased rapidly during the late 1940's and early 1950's, reaching its peak in 1953. The peak net migration rate of 1953 was sufficiently large to exceed the rate of natural increase and cause a reduction in the absolute population. Subtracting the net migration rate from the rate of natural increase gives the actual rate of population increase per thousand, which is presented in Table 3.1, column 6. Figure 3.2 illustrates the significant impact of migration and its success in reducing the rate of population growth from an explosive to a moderate one in the period 1940–1950 and to an abnormally low rate for the period 1950–1960. The large divergence between the trend of birth minus death rates and the trend of births minus deaths and emigration is easily observed from the chart for the period 1940–1962. The gap between the two trends would have been even larger if the birth rate had not declined (in part, due to migration) during the same period of time.

Population Estimates

In order to examine the real impact of emigration on population growth it is necessary to compare the actual population growth with estimates of the expected growth without emigration and a declining birth rate. Table 3.3 presents two estimates of population growth plus the actual growth in Puerto Rico for the period 1940–1962. The estimate in column 3, B-1, assumed the absence of emigration and the continuation of the high birth rate existing during the early 1940's, that is, 40 per thousand. The estimate in column 4 also assumed the absence of emigration and the continuation of the high fertility rate, that is, 180 per thousand women 15–44, that prevailed during the early 1940's. The latter estimate is larger than B-1, the former, as a result of the greater proportion of emigrants in the age bracket 15–44. A comparison of the actual population A-1 with the highest estimate of the expected population C-1 indicates that an additional 1,312,000 more people would have been living on the crowded island, or approximately 53 per cent more people than were on the island in 1962.

Translating the population figures into growth rates for the two decades and for the entire twenty-two year period provides an additional perspective to the type of population problem that would have existed without emigration and the concomitant fall in the birth rate. Table 3.4 reveals that the greatest difference in popula-

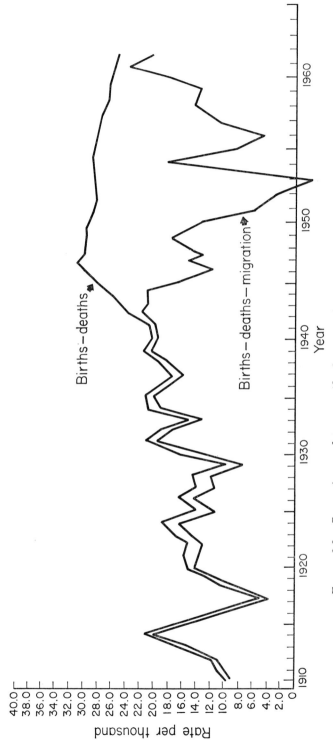

FIGURE 3.2. *Rates of natural increase (births minus deaths) and population increase (births minus deaths minus migration) in Puerto Rico 1910–1963.*

TABLE 3.3

ACTUAL AND ESTIMATED PUERTO RICAN POPULATION ANNUALLY
1940–1960

(All rates are per thousand population)

Year	Actual Population A-1	Estimated Population B-1	Estimated Population C-1
1940	1,878	1,878	1,878
1941	1,912	1,914	1,920
1942	1,946	1,950	1,963
1943	1,980	1,992	2,011
1944	2,014	2,038	2,066
1945	2,049	2,102	2,132
1946	2,083	2,173	2,198
1947	2,117	2,239	2,267
1948	2,151	2,301	2,339
1949	2,185	2,375	2,413
1950	2,218	2,458	2,492
1951	2,224	2,532	2,580
1952	2,202	2,603	2,674
1953	2,132	2,642	2,778
1954	2,195	2,706	2,873
1955	2,235	2,819	2,982
1956	2,237	2,894	3,095
1957	2,252	2,954	3,208
1958	2,295	3,058	3,322
1959	2,321	3,132	3,437
1960	2,358	3,207	3,549
1961	2,404	3,289	3,660
1962	2,455	3,376	3,767

Source: Column 1, Commonwealth of Puerto Rico, Department of Health, Division of Demographic Registry and Vital Statistics, *Annual Vital Statistics Report* (San Juan, Commonwealth of Puerto Rico, 1962).
The method of estimating population B-1 and C-1 is described in the text.

tion growth rates between the C-1 estimate and the actual population occurred in the 1950–1960 period. The expected population growth rate in that decade was a very high 3.5 per cent per annum, while the actual population growth rate was one of the lowest in the world — 0.6 per cent per annum.

The obvious conclusion is that Puerto Rican emigration was of sufficient magnitude to reduce an extremely high population growth rate to an insignificant and negligible level. The rate of actual population growth for the period 1940–1962 averaged approximately 1.2 per cent per annum compared to the estimated rate of growth of 3.3 per cent per annum. This represents a reduction in the expected population growth of approximately 67 per cent in a little

TABLE 3.4

RATES OF PUERTO RICAN POPULATION GROWTH FOR SELECTED PERIODS
(*Percentages*)

Period	Rate of Actual Population Growth per Annum A-1	Rate of Estimated Population Growth per Annum C-1
1940–1962	1.2	3.3
1940–1950	1.7	2.9
1950–1960	0.6	3.5

Estimated Population Growth C-1 assumed the elimination of all emigration and the continuation of the high fertility rate that prevailed in the mid-1940's.

Source: United States Department of Commerce, Bureau of the Census, *Census of Population: 1960, Characteristics of the Population*, Parts 51–54, Volume II (Washington, D. C.: United States Government Printing Office, 1961).

more than two decades. Perloff's fear of the danger of rapid population growth in Puerto Rico was justified. He stated in 1948 that

> within the limits of our present knowledge, it can be said that Puerto Rico cannot hope to achieve higher levels of living or, possibly, even to maintain its present level of living over a long period of time without an integrated program aimed at checking the very rapid rate of population growth.[14]

Fortunately for Puerto Rico, emigration was an effective substitute for an integrated program to check the population growth of the island. The voluntary movement of large numbers of the population was an effective method of reducing the obstacle of rapid population growth, thus enabling output growth to be translated into improvements in the standard of living of the remaining Puerto Rican population. As the size and rate of migration decrease, the determination of future population growth will be controlled by the direction and rate of change in the birth rate. If the birth rate rises in the future, the gains in per capita income and standards of living will be severely retarded.

The Birth Rate Trend

Although migration directly accounted for the decline in the expected population growth, the decline in the birth rate also con-

[14] *Ibid.*, p. 208.

tributed significantly. However, the cause of the declining birth rate is directly linked to the large-scale emigration. The existence of a large proportion of emigrants in the reproductive age bracket 15–44 resulted in a lower percentage and number of reproductive members of the society and thus contributed to the decline in the birth rate per thousand. Even with the declining birth rate trend, without emigration there would have been an additional 900,000 people living in Puerto Rico in 1962. This reflects the fact that had they stayed the emigrants directly, without changes in assumptions of the birth rate and the causes of the decline, would have accounted for an additional 37 per cent of the 53 per cent increase in the population. The contribution of the birth rate decline would be the residual of the percentage increase of the difference between actual and expected population growth under the assumption of no change in birth rates, or a 16 per cent decrease due to declining birth rates.

The actual decline in the birth rate is described in Table 3.1, column 2. The turning point from a rising to a declining birth rate occurred in 1947–1948. The rate moved from an all-time high of 43.2 per thousand to its current low of 30.9 per thousand. This decrease represents a drop of 28.5 per cent in a fifteen-year period. The statistics indicate that the rate of decrease of the birth rate from 1947 onward was greater than the rate of decrease of the death rate, causing a decrease in the rate of natural increase throughout the period 1947–1962. Even though the lag between the falling death and birth rates was unusually short (seven years) and the decrease in the birth rate exceeded that of the death rate, this was not sufficient to prevent rapid increases in the population in the short run. The rate of natural increase still remained moderately high — 24.2 per thousand in 1962. Large-scale emigration was necessary in reducing the rate of population growth during the crucial stage of economic development.

Relating these statistics to the theoretical discussion, with growth in output in Puerto Rico ranging from 0.6 to 2.5 per cent per annum, we find that there would have been no gains in per capita income without emigration. Since the rate of effective migration prevailing during this period reduced the population growth to 0.6 per cent per annum, even a low rate of output growth — that is, any rate above 0.6 per cent — would have resulted in a higher rate of growth of per capita income instead of stagnation or a declining level of per capita income.

The importance of the duration of the time lag between the fall-

ing birth and death rates cannot be ignored. The longer the time
lag between the two declining rates, the more rapid the growth of
future population. Thus, any measures which effectively reduce the
lag will have a significant impact on the size and rate of growth of
the future population. The greater number of births create a wider
base of the population pyramid and thus more reproductive people
in the next generation, resulting in even more rapid rates of population growth. A smaller time lag between the decline in the death
rate and the decline in the birth rate (even though the death-rate
decline is greater than the birth-rate decline) contributes to the
reduction of the base of the population pyramid and reduces the
population growth of the future. The significance of the short time
lag between the fall in the death and birth rates experienced in
Puerto Rico will be evident in the lowered population growth rates
observed in future years on the island.

Effects of Emigration on the Age Structure of the Population

The age structure of a population is an important determinant
of its future rate of growth. G. Sundbärg was the first to observe
the relationship between age structure and the rate of population
growth. He classified populations into three distinct types:

  a. progressive, having a high proportion of children and a high rate
      of growth;
  b. stationary, having moderate proportions of children and aged per-
      sons with a slow growth or stationary numbers;
  c. regressive, having a high proportion of aged persons and declining
      numbers.[15]

As I postulated in Chapter 2, the occurrence of large-scale emigration concentrated in a short period of time will have a strong
impact on the age structure of the population if the age structure
distribution among the migrants is different from the distribution
of the remaining population.

An examination of the impact of the Puerto Rican emigration on
the age structure of the population reveals that a significant decrease occurred in all age groups from 1–60, with the largest decrease in the age bracket 15–44. Eighty-five per cent of those who
emigrated were in the age bracket 15–44,[16] while this group com-

---

[15] United Nations, Population Study No. 17, op. cit., p. 141.
[16] This figure was calculated from the estimate of the population without

posed just 42 per cent of the population of Puerto Rico.[17] The large differences between the age distributions of the Puerto Rican and migrant populations account for the major changes that occurred in the age structure.

In order to obtain a complete picture of the total effect of emigration on the age structure of the population, a projection of the expected age structure without emigration was calculated and is presented in Table 3.5, along with the actual age structure for 1960. The difference between the estimated and the actual age structure indicates the areas of greatest change resulting from emigration, for each age group and for the total age structure. (Column 4 contains the actual differences.) The estimated population structure was calculated by projecting the number of people in the age brackets 0–20 in 1950 forward ten years and then reducing this number for each age category by the age-specific mortality rates during the decade of the 1950's. For the age brackets 20-plus the same procedure was employed except that the base year was 1940 and the projections and mortality adjustments extended over a twenty-year period.

This method of estimation indicated a decrease in the total number of people during the period 1940–1960 of 577,994, and the estimate compared almost perfectly with the migration statistics, which indicate a departure of 578,000. The number of additional people aged 15–44 who would have been in the population in 1960 amounted to 491,000, and their loss thus caused a substantial reduction in the reproductive population. In percentage terms it represented a loss of 34 per cent of the total number of people in the 15–44 age category. This provides evidence supporting the hypothesis that the emigration contains a large segment of the reproductive population and generally the younger portion of the population.

---

emigration, compared to the estimate with emigration. The results of the comparison are presented in Table 3.5. Additional confirmation of the percentage was obtained from the ramp survey conducted at the airport in San Juan for a sample of passengers arriving and departing Puerto Rico for the years 1957 to the present. The latter information can be found in the report published by the Commonwealth of Puerto Rico, Department of Labor, Bureau of Labor Statistics, *Characteristics of Passengers Who Traveled by Air Between Puerto Rico and the United States* (San Juan, Commonwealth of Puerto Rico, 1957–1962).

[17] United States Department of Commerce, Bureau of the Census, *Census of Population: 1950, Characteristics of the Population*, Parts 51–14, Vol. II (Washington, D. C.: United States Government Printing Office, 1953), pp. 53–30.

TABLE 3.5

EFFECT OF EMIGRATION ON THE AGE STRUCTURE OF
THE PUERTO RICAN POPULATION 1940–1960

Age	Estimated Population 1960	Actual Population 1960	Difference Resulting from Emigration
0–4	371,753	355,700	16,063
5–9	385,531	328,700	56,831
10–14	349,687	321,207	28,497
15–19	315,602	246,860	68,742
20–24	256,400	171,655	84,785
25–29	241,027	136,190	104,837
30–34	214,472	126,729	87,743
35–39	191,524	130,664	61,060
40–44	190,201	107,357	82,848
45–49	129,000	105,588	23,412
50–54	81,646	75,208	6,438
55–59	74,638	65,872	8,766
60–64	58,972	58,070	902
65–69	41,506	48,104	+ 6,482
70–74	25,741	31,504	+ 5,763
75–79	2,690	21,236	+ 18,546
80–84	1,137	10,124	+ 9,887

The method of estimating the 1960 age-specific population of Puerto Rico is described in the text. It is interesting to note that the actual number of people above 65 years of age (column 4) was greater than the estimate of expected population in these age brackets. Several factors can account for this increase — namely, the return migration of elderly people who seek retirement in their native country, the underreporting of mortality rates for these age categories, and the retirement of foreign-born people.

Source: United States Department of Commerce, Bureau of the Census, *Census of Population: 1960, Puerto Rico, Detailed Characteristics of the Population* (Washington, D. C.: United States Government Printing Office, 1961).

Since all age groups below 65 decreased in number, the growth of the population during this period must be explained by the increased number of children below ten years of age, that is, those born in the decade of the 1950's, and the increase in the number of elderly people above 65 years of age.

The large movement of people in the age bracket 15–44 resulted in a decrease in the percentage of the population in that age bracket from 45.4 per cent in 1940 to 39.2 per cent in 1960, or a decline of 6.2 per cent. This type of direct calculation understates the significance of the actual decline. A better indication of the decline can be obtained by comparing the expected percentage with the actual percentage. The percentage of people 15–44 in the estimated population was 48.1; in the actual population it was 39.2 per cent. This represents a decrease of 9.0 per cent from emigration (a percentage decrease of 18.6 per cent) compared to a decrease of only 13.5 per cent in the same age group between 1940 and 1960. In either case the evidence is clear; emigration significantly reduced the proportion and number of people in the reproductive age categories. The largest reduction in an age group occurred for those 20–24, decreasing from 11.0 per cent in 1940 to 7.3 per cent in 1960, or almost 33 per cent. This substantiates the hypothesis that the migration stream consists of young reproductive members of the population.

With regard to future population growth, the effect of emigration on the age structure resulted in a decrease in the base of the pyramid: fewer children, a larger decrease in the reproductive members, less young adults, and an increase in the number of elderly people. According to G. Sundbärg's classifications, it moved the future growth of Puerto Rican population from a progressive one to one approaching a more stationary type. This effect on the age structure will reduce the rate of population growth in Puerto Rico in future generations significantly from the rates that would have resulted had there been no emigration. In conclusion, it appears that emigration not only had a profound effect on reducing the population growth in the short run but via its impact on the age structure had a positive effect of reducing the long-run potential growth of the Puerto Rican population.

Changes in the Fertility Pattern in Puerto Rico

The sharp decline of the birth rate is further accentuated when contrasted with the birth rate declines in other countries. For example:

> It took France over seventy years to experience a drop in her birth rate from 30 to 20 per thousand, while this process lasted about forty years in Sweden and Switzerland and about thirty years in England and Denmark.[18]

The decline of the birth rate in Puerto Rico is a clearly documented fact. However, there is still a great deal of controversy as to whether the decline represents a general and pervasive attempt by the population to restrict consciously and rationally family size or whether it is purely a statistical phenomenon representing a reduction of

[18] United Nations, Population Study No. 17, *op. cit.*, p. 72.

the reproductive members of the population, which has caused a lowering of the birth rate. It is the objective of this section of the chapter to examine what changes have occurred with regard to the fertility pattern of the Puerto Rican society.

Two separate reports prepared under the auspices of different agencies of the Puerto Rican government[19] conclude that the decline in the birth rates was primarily due to the large amount of migration containing a large portion of the reproductive age groups of the Puerto Rican population. Most significantly, both reports also concluded that the high fertility rates existing throughout the period prior to 1950 still exist in the 1960's. One of the reports[20] contains the fertility rates for each sex for 1950 and 1960. The figures are presented in Table 3.6, along with my own calculations of different age-sex fertility rates in parentheses below the figures. The government's report indicates that there was a small increase in the "effective fertility" of women in the age range 15–39; and among the men in the age range 20–44 the effective fertility was considerably higher at the end of the decade than at the beginning. The report does indicate that the reduction in infant mortality, from 5,787 in 1949 to 3,555 in 1950, accounts for part of this apparent increase in effective fertility. The report summarizes the current situation as follows:

> Maintenance of high fertility rates during the 1950's has serious implications for future population growth. It means that the decline in the birth rate during the 1950's was largely, if not entirely, the result of migration of relatively large numbers of young adults. A reduction of migration during the 1960's might halt or even reverse the decline in the birth rate.[21]

The second government report reaffirms the pessimism of the conclusions of the first report with a gloomy forecast:

[19] Commonwealth of Puerto Rico, Fourth Legislative Assembly, Joint Committee of Socio-Economic Research, *Population Changes Outside the San Juan Metropolitan Area, 1950-1960* (San Juan, Commonwealth of Puerto Rico, 1960). The second report will be part of a doctoral dissertation by José L. Vazquez at the University of Chicago, "The Demographic Evolution of Puerto Rico and Its Transfer Value for Other Underdeveloped Areas." The report was prepared under the auspices of the section of Biostatistics, Department of Preventive Medicine and Public Health (San Juan, Commonwealth of Puerto Rico, 1963).

[20] Joint Committee on Socio-Economic Research, *op. cit.*, p. 21.

[21] *Ibid.*, p. 26.

As in the case of Japan, industrialization has failed to produce detectable changes in the reproductive performance of the island's population.[22]

Contrary to these pessimistic conclusions about the future of population growth in Puerto Rico, there is strong evidence that fertility rates since 1947 have definitely decreased and that this decline is clearly associated with the industrialization and economic growth of the island. These findings, based on additional information and calculations, should provide the basis for a more optimistic outlook on the population problems of Puerto Rico.

The calculations of different fertility rates presented in Table 3.6 are based on the number of live births and do not reflect effective fertility rates, which are a function of the number of surviving infants, zero to one year old. The use of the statistics of live births provides a better indication of the number of conceptions than the number of infants zero to one. It is conceded that effective fertility provides a better estimate of the growth of future population growth problems, but it does not reflect the actual fertility pattern changes of a population.

The results of the calculations of fertility rates using live birth statistics are startling when contrasted to the conclusions of the two government reports which used effective fertility rates. In every category of age and sex the data indicate a decline in fertility rates for the period 1950–1960. If we compare the change during the ten-year period of fertility rates of females 15–39, using live births, with the effective fertility rates, the differences are quite marked. The fertility rate of this category dropped 7 per cent, from 201 to 187, while the effective fertility rate increased from 167 to 178, or 6 per cent. The fertility rate for males 20–44 decreased the least of all categories, from 245 to 241, or 2 per cent, during the ten-year period. The effective fertility rate for the same category of males increased from 204 to 241, or 18 per cent.

One of the major reasons why the male fertility rate exceeded the female fertility rate was that a larger number of males in the reproductive age groups 15–44 emigrated than females. Another reason is that the percentage of married males between 15–35 increased. For example, in 1950 only 30.8 per cent of the males 20–24 were married, compared to 36.4 per cent in 1960. For the age bracket

22 Vazquez, *op. cit.*, Chapter 8, p. 3.

TABLE 3.6

AGE-SEX FERTILITY RATES IN PUERTO RICO FOR SELECTED YEARS*

(*All rates are per thousand population*)

Age-Sex	1960	1950	1940
Males 15–44	437,776	457,829	420,467
Fertility Rate	(174)	(187)	(172)
Males 15–39	384,680	410,077	376,728
Fertility Rate	(198)	(208)	(192)
Males 20–44	315,165	348,915	321,007
Fertility Rate	(241)	(245)	(226)
Females 15–44	481,694	469,407	429,722
Fertility Rate	(158)	(182)	(168)
Females 15–39	427,428	425,922	387,489
Fertility Rate	(178)	(201)	(187)
Females 20–44	357,436	358,091	323,033
Fertility Rate	(213)	(239)	(224)
Total 15–44	919,470	927,236	850,239
Fertility Rate	(83)	(92)	(85)
Total 15–39	812,160	835,999	764,217
Fertility Rate	(94)	(102)	(95)
Total 20–44	672,601	707,005	644,040
Fertility Rate	(113)	(121)	(112)
Males 20–44 and			
Females 15–39	742,593	774,836	708,496
Fertility Rate	(102)	(110)	(102)
"Effective" Fertility Rate			
Males 20–44	(241)	(204)	
and			
Females 15–39	(178)	(167)	

Source: United States Department of Commerce, Bureau of the Census, *Census of Population: 1960 and 1950, Puerto Rico, Detailed Characteristics of the Population* (Washington, D. C.: United States Government Printing Office, 1951 and 1961).

* The figures in parentheses are the author's.

25–29, only 65.1 per cent were married in 1950, compared to 71.0 per cent in 1960. The emigration of males in these age groups was a factor in raising the percentages of young married males in Puerto Rico. This increased marriage rate and the reduction in the number of reproductive males naturally contributed to a higher fertility rate of males than females.

When combining the age groups above for both sexes, the fertility rates show a decline from a rate of 110 in 1950 to 102 in 1960, or 7.3 per cent. The likelihood of an underenumeration of live births in the 1950 census suggests an even greater decrease in the actual fertility pattern during the ten-year period. In order to obtain a more complete examination of the changes in the fertility patterns of the entire society, it seems desirable to enlarge the age-sex categories to include the larger proportion of reproductive population, that is, all people 15–44. The calculations of these fertility rates are presented in Table 3.6, line 7. The fertility rate for people 15–44 increased from 83 in 1940 to 92 in 1950 and then decreased to 85 in 1960. The underenumeration of live births in the earlier census years and the reduction in the number of foetal deaths during pregnancy and infant deaths during delivery in the two decades results in an underestimation of the actual fertility rate decreases during the twenty-year period. Aside from this problem, the decline in fertility rates represented a 10 per cent decrease in the 1950–1960 period. These data support the position that the fertility pattern in Puerto Rico did undergo a significant change during the 1950–1960 period. This change will be more significant if we compare it to an estimate of the expected fertility rate in 1960 had the trend in the 1940's persisted throughout the 1950's. The expected rate of fertility in 1960 would have been 100, compared to the actual rate of 85, a 15 per cent decrease within one decade. Clearly, this is a profound and significant change in the fertility pattern of the Puerto Rican society.

Economic Growth and Fertility Patterns

What factors influenced or were associated with the decline in the Puerto Rican fertility rate during the period 1950–1960? Did industrialization or economic growth play an influential role in affecting the fertility pattern? The relationship between economic growth and the changes in demographic variables (fertility and mortality) is still controversial, and additional empirical studies are needed to clarify the relationships. With the rate of emigration from Puerto Rico tapering off rapidly in the first three years of the 1960's, the major determinant of population growth will be the rate of change and the direction of the fertility rates. If fertility factors are independent of economic variables, then Puerto Rico's future population growth will not be influenced or controlled by rapid economic growth. There would be no assurance that population growth would not continue to absorb the gains in output and thus prevent improvements in the per capita income of the population. On the other hand, if there is a close relationship between economic growth and fertility patterns, as is hypothesized in the theoretical discussion, then as the economic system expands, it will provide a built-in mechanism reducing fertility rates and thus preventing the growth of population.

My theoretical framework included a hypothesis that the birth rate (also fertility rate) was a function of the level of per capita income. At low per capita incomes additional increases in income may stimulate increases in the birth and fertility rates. The increase in births is primarily attributed to greater ability to support a larger family. However, after a minimum threshold per capita income is attained, further increases in income per capita result in decreases in the birth and fertility rates. In other words, a positive relationship exists between income per capita and birth rates at low levels of income and an inverse relationship emerges after a threshold income per capita is attained. Associated with this threshold per capita income is a variety of changes brought about by rapid economic growth, specifically: (a) higher educational attainment of the population; (b) greater knowledge and awareness of methods of family control and planning; (c) a greater degree of rationality in decision making; (d) awareness and experience of the ability to control one's natural environment; (e) higher costs of rearing additional children; (f) changing role of women in the society; and (g) increased urbanization. These changes exert a profound and fundamental impact on traditional values and attitudes of the population, which in turn change attitudes and actions with regard to family size. Eventually these changes are reflected in the declining trends in fertility rates observed in many countries as economic growth proceeds.

The data on birth rates and per capita income of Puerto Rico are presented in Appendix B; they reveal the parallel movements of both variables from 1940–1947, with a structural change occurring in 1947. After this date income per capita continued to increase rapidly while the birth rate and fertility rate reversed their direction and decreased continuously until 1963. This movement tends to support my hypothesis.

In order to test the hypothesis that economic growth exerts a strong influence on the fertility rates, a multiple regression analysis of the annual levels of fertility and birth rates was attempted to observe the influence of a set of independent variables representing economic growth on both the birth and fertility rates[23] during the 1947–1962 period. Both of the regression equations had the same independent variables: income per capita, education, female labor force participation rates, and the number of people in the age bracket 15–44. This variable was included because its change after the wave of emigration was thought to be the dominant cause of the reduced birth rate in the 1950–1960 period. The analysis would reveal what impact the decline in the number of reproductive people had on birth rates compared to the impact of the other independent variables. An inverse relationship was expected between the two separate dependent variables and the independent variables, with the exception of a positive relationship expected between the birth rate and the number of people 15–44 in the population.

If the expected relationships emerge, any favorable effect of emigration on the important independent variables would indicate that emigration had a positive indirect effect on reducing the fertility rates in Puerto Rico. The level and rate of growth of per capita income will be determined, in part, by the size and rate of emigration. Educational attainment of the population may increase if the uneducated comprise the bulk of the migration stream and/or if greater educational opportunities are now available to the remaining population, given the allocation of limited educational expenditures. This would result in greater expenditures per child, which would allow faster increases in the educational attainment of the population. Emigration may affect the number of women in the labor force, depending on whether there is a greater proportion of female labor force numbers in the migration stream compared to the economy. Last, the emigration to the United States may stimulate internal migration from rural to urban areas within Puerto Rico, or it may shift the proportions of population residing in urban and rural areas, depending on where the migrants resided in Puerto Rico.

Emigration can have a direct influence on each of the independent variables; and if, in turn, the independent variables are associated with and/or explain decreases in the dependent vari-

[23] The analysis of both the birth and fertility rates in Puerto Rico appears redundant. The birth rate was included because there is a consensus and a well-documented empirical fact that the birth rate has declined. The fertility rates were estimated and thus may be subject to either error or question as to their decline. The method of estimation is described in the text.

ables, emigration has indirectly contributed to the changing fertility pattern in Puerto Rico.

A Regression Model

The regression equations for fertility and birth rate analysis took the following form:

$$X = C + a_1(Y) + a_2(E) + a_3(F) + a_4(U) + a_5(P)$$

(3.1)

$$Z = C + a_1(Y) + a_2(E) + a_3(F) + a_4(U)$$

(3.2)

where X = birth rate, Z = fertility rate, C = constant term, $a_1 \cdots a_5$ = the coefficients of the independent variables, Y = per capita income, E = education, F = female labor force participation rate, U = urbanizaiton, P = number of people 15–44 in the population.

Recent studies[24] of fertility patterns provide a firm basis for expecting an inverse relationship between per capita income and fertility rates. Beside the changing attitude and values accompanying rising incomes, higher income provides both the means to purchase contraceptive materials and greater access to doctors and information. These factors increase the ability of individuals to transform desires into action — that is, to restrict the size of their families. Thus it is expected that as per capita incomes increase during the development of the economy, fertility rates will begin to decline in response to rising incomes. Real disposable income per capita was selected, but it was lagged one year in order to reflect the income level at the time of conception.

Although income and educational levels are highly correlated, it is necessary to include education as an independent variable having a significant effect on fertility regardless of the income level. A study of Puerto Rican mothers with different incomes and education was undertaken in 1946. The important conclusion that emerged was that mothers with high incomes and more than eight grades of education had significantly fewer numbers of children

---

[24] Irma Adelman, "An Econometric Analysis of Population Growth," *American Economic Review*, Vol. LIII, No. 3 (June 1963), pp. 314–339. This article contains an interesting analysis of fertility and mortality and economic growth for a number of countries on a cross-section analysis. The study indicates an inverse relationship, emerging slowly as the economy grows, between fertility rates and per capita incomes. The article also contains numerous references citing the relationships found between economic growth and fertility.

compared to women with high incomes and low educational attainments.[25]

On the basis of this study, a separate educational variable was included in the analysis. The changes in attitudes, knowledge, awareness, rationality are all products of an education that should exert significant influence on the decision of family size. The study indicated that at least a sixth-grade education was necessary before significant differences among the number of children born to a mother emerged. With this in mind, the education variable selected was the number of students enrolled in junior and senior high schools, projected five years into the future. This was considered a good proxy variable for arriving at some estimation of the number of people in the reproductive age brackets 15–44 who had at least six grades or more of schooling. The greater the percentage of the reproductive population with this amount of education, the greater the effect on the fertility rates of this group. An exact estimate of the educational attainment of this group was not available on an annual basis. After a five-year projection, all the pupils enrolled in junior and senior high shoools would have been in the age bracket 15–44.

Higher rates of female labor force participation were expected to exert a negative influence on the fertility rate because of several factors: (a) greater amounts of time devoted to activities away from home; (b) less time for, and increased cost of, rearing chil-

---

[25] The unpublished study, "Patterns of Living in Puerto Rican Families" (University of Puerto Rico, 1948), was under the direction of Dr. Lydia Roberts. Fortunately some of the findings are presented in Perloff, op. cit., p. 213. The following relationship between level of education and number of children per mother was discovered:

Level of Schooling of Mothers	Number of Children per Mother
No formal schooling	6.1
1 or 2 grades	5.0
3, 4, 5 grades	4.6
6, 7, 8 grades	3.4
Completion of high school	2.4

A study undertaken by Jaffe found data that conformed to the first study. For example, mothers with less than five grades of education had an average of 4.25 children; five to nine grades, 3.58 children; and mothers with ten or more grades had an average of 2.20 children. An interesting and detailed discussion on education and fertility can be found in A. J. Jaffe, *People, Jobs and Economic Development* (Glencoe, Ill.: Free Press, 1959), pp. 180–184.

Both Perloff and Jaffe stress the importance of education as an essential aspect of controlling the future birth rate in Puerto Rico.

dren; (c) changing attitudes toward women resulting in more status and a greater amount of decision making; (d) older marriage ages; and (e) higher educational attainment of women in order to secure industrial jobs.

Urbanization has been associated with sharp decreases in fertility rates in many countries.[26] The additional costs of rearing children in cities compared to rural areas should exert a strong influence on fertility rates. The economic usefulness of child labor in rural farm areas is one of the reasons offered for rural families having greater numbers of children than urban families. The host of associated changes that emerge with rapid urbanization, such as (a) reduction in living space; (b) increased costs of housing, transportation, and food; (c) changing values; and (d) closer contact with other social and economic groups — all help to reduce the fertility rates in urban areas. Actual figures for the ratio of urban to rural dwellers were not available on a yearly basis. As a substitute for the actual figures, the amount of agricultural employment as a percentage of total employment was used. This percentage should reflect the decline in the number and percentage of people living in rural areas because agricultural employment is the dominant means of earning a living in the rural locations.

The argument that emigration of the reproductive members of the population was the cause of the declining birth rate in Puerto Rico needed to be examined carefully. Therefore, the birth rate analysis includes a variable reflecting the population in the age bracket 15–44 for each year. This variable was also necessary in order to calculate annual fertility rates. Unfortunately, there was no yearly tabulation of people aged 15–44. An estimation was obtained by using the census year figures for this age group as benchmarks, varying the weights for each year according to the distance from the two benchmark years, and then adjusting for the migration of the people in this age bracket each year. For example, the figure arrived at for 1949 was composed of nine tenths of the 1950 figure and one tenth of the 1940 figure, adjusted for the number in the 15–44 age category who migrated that year. The fertility rates based on this estimate are presented in Appendix B along with the changes in the independent variables and the birth rate.

[26] United Nations, Population Study No. 17, *op. cit.*, contains an account of the factors affecting fertility rates and the studies of different fertility rates in urban *versus* rural areas.

Regression Results

The results of the multiple regression analysis of the Puerto Rican birth rate indicate that the five independent variables yielded an excellent fit for explaining the variance of the birth rate during the period 1947–1962. The equation yielded the following results:

$$X = 32.5 - .015(Y) - .097(E) + .037(F) - .147(U) + .022(P)$$
$$(.011) \quad (.036) \quad (.167) \quad (.176) \quad (.011)$$

$$(3.1a)$$

The regression fit gave an R^2 of .976 and an R (multiple correlation coefficient) corrected for degrees of freedom of .988. In contrast to the excellent fit, only two variables — education and 15–44 population — had statistically significant coefficients. All the expected signs of the independent variables emerged with the exception of the female labor force participation rate, which had a positive relationship with birth rates.

When urbanization and female labor force participation rates are eliminated from the equation, the multiple regression yields almost the same excellent fit:

$$X = 30.2 - .015(Y) - .065(E) + .018(P)$$
$$(.011) \quad (.024) \quad (.009)$$

$$(3.1b)$$

with an R corrected for degrees of freedom of .980 and an R^2 of .960. The similar R^2's for the two regressions indicate that the two variables left out of Equation 3.1b were not useful in explaining the variance in the birth rate. The income per capita variable did not have a significant coefficient. This may be partly attributable to the close correlation between the education and income variables. Moreover, when regressing birth rates only on per capita income, it also provides a very good fit with an R^2 of .952. The coefficient of income per capita now emerges as significant $(-.045(Y); (.001))$. The close correlation between income per capita and education can be seen when regressing birth rates only on the education variable. Again, a very good fit emerges with an R^2 of .947, and the coefficient of education is also statistically significant. Thus, either variable alone provides a good least-squares fit for birth rates during the period 1947–1962.

The partial correlation coefficients of the regressed variables in Equation 3.1*b* were $Y = -.386$, $E = -.624$, and $P = +.506$. The high degree of collinearity between education and income reduces the partial correlation of each of the variables. Eliminating either one of the two variables results in very high partial correlation coefficients for the other (for all the regressions all the partial correlation coefficients for each one was above .90).

An attempt was made to substitute a different variable for estimating the educational attainment of the reproductive population. The variable selected was the ratio of skilled to unskilled workers. The equations including this variable did not provide better results. In most of the regression equations the skilled worker ratio did not have a significant coefficient, nor did it possess the expected negative sign as the other education variable had. Apparently, the lumping of skill categories reduces the level of education significantly in the skilled groups, so that the education levels between the two groups are not large enough to discriminate differences among the two different occupational groups. Thus, the first education variable provided a better proxy variable for the estimate of the educational attainment of the reproductive population.

Quite similar results were obtained for the multiple regression analysis of fertility rates for the period 1947–1962. The least-squares estimate yielded

$$Z = 127.2 - .039(Y) - .147(E) + .025(F) - .477(U)$$
$$\quad\quad\quad (.023)\quad\quad (.073)\quad\quad (.503)\quad\quad (.507)$$

$$(3.2b)$$

with an R corrected for degrees of freedom of .963 and an R^2 of .927. All the expected signs emerged with the exception of the female labor force participation rate.

The female labor force participation rate did not increase in Puerto Rico. A large number of female migrants were labor force members, thus reducing the actual number and percentage of female labor force members. If the migration had not occurred, industrialization would have stimulated a greater female labor force and the rate would have risen during the time that the fertility and birth rate decreased, thus giving an inverse relationship instead of the positive one observed from the regression results.

Regressing fertility rates on lagged real disposable personal income per capita gives a very good least-squares fit:

$$Z = 110.2 - .074(Y)$$
$$(.005)$$

$$(3.2b)$$

with an R corrected for degrees of freedom of .955 and an R^2 of .912.

Qualifications

One fundamental weakness of the multiple regression analysis is that most of the variables did not have significant coefficients. A large part of the problem stems from the similar movements of the variables through time. In other words, the trends are clear, without significant variations, and it is difficult to isolate causation with such a phenomenon occurring among both the dependent and independent variables. The statistical data in Appendix B indicate clearly the trend problem among the variables selected in the regression equation. Although a strong conclusion regarding causation cannot be drawn from the statistical analysis above, it is clear that economic growth is closely associated with the declining birth and fertility rates in Puerto Rico. The high correlations between birth and fertility rates and either income per capita or education reflect the close association.

A cross-section analysis of fertility rates by municipality in Puerto Rico in 1950 provided additional data supporting the inverse relationship between education and per capita income with birth and fertility rates. A calculation of fertility rates was undertaken for all the municipalities in Puerto Rico. A comparison of the high and low fertility municipalities with respect to education and income provided the following conclusion: education and income levels were significantly higher in low fertility areas than in high fertility areas. Specifically, in the eleven municipalities with the highest fertility rates on the island, the mean income per capita was $284 while in the eleven municipalities with the lowest fertility rates the mean income was $476.

With regard to education, in the same high fertility areas the percentage of females who completed eight grades of school or more was 8.3, compared to 17.4 in the low fertility areas. Comparing the mean grade of education completed by females gives a similar finding — 2.0 for the high fertility areas and 3.5 for the low areas. The education of males resulted in similar findings with slightly higher grades and percentages for each category.

These additional data suggest that higher education combined with higher per capita income are clearly associated with lower fertility rates.

The conclusion of the statistical analysis indicates that as the economy of the island grows, it is quite likely that the fertility pattern will continue to decrease. The association between the economic growth variables and fertility rates is significantly close to suggest some definite causation. Further cross-section analysis would be required to isolate the amount of causation of the decline in fertility resulting from economic growth. In any event, it appears that future population growth will be reduced on the island provided that the economy and the education and income per capita levels of the population continue to increase.

The importance of female education as a positive factor controlling the fertility rates should stimulate an evaluation of the allocation of resources invested in the primary educational schools in many underdeveloped, overpopulated economies. The desire to control future population growth in order to maximize the rate of growth of per capita income may require additional calculations on the returns from education, particularly primary education. Apparently, the decision by Governor Muñoz-Marín to provide universal education to all the people of Puerto Rico on humanitarian grounds may have had the extra by-product of an internal mechanism reducing fertility rates and future population growth on the island. The residual allocation of the government's budget to education may be too little and not the most economical in the long run, especially in countries facing serious population pressure.

Summary

The analysis of the effects of emigration provide substantial evidence that emigration succeeded in controlling and reducing the population growth of Puerto Rico in the short and long run. The migration was of such significant size that it reduced the population growth from a potential rate of over 3 per cent to a low rate of 0.6 per cent. In addition, it withdrew large segments of the reproductive population, hollowing out the age group 15–44 and causing a lower rate of births in the future.

The withdrawal of large numbers of people probably contributed to the rapid rate of increase in per capita income, which was closely associated with the declining fertility rates observed in

Puerto Rico since 1947. This reduction reflects a fundamental change in the fertility pattern of the society, which will prevent rapid population growth as long as the trend continues to exist.

In conclusion, emigration provided an excellent safety valve mechanism for the solution of a very serious and dangerous population problem. Without the large-scale emigration, the island of Puerto Rico would have been overburdened with the attempt to support an additional 1,300,000 people and even greater numbers with more rapid increases in the future decades. In this particular case, emigration was a practical and successful method of coping with a population problem and thus allowing for rapid gains in per capita income and the standard of living during the past two decades in Puerto Rico.

4

The Effects of Emigration on the Puerto Rican Labor Force

Introduction

A change in the size and quality of the labor force has an important effect on the growth of output and productivity. Thus, in order to assess the effect of emigration on the growth of output and productivity in Puerto Rico, it is necessary to analyze the impact of emigration on the size and quality of the labor force. The large-scale exodus of thousands of Puerto Ricans to the United States in a short period of time, 1945–1960, had a significant impact on the size and composition of the Puerto Rican population. A migration stream stimulated by economic forces, differentials in earnings, and unemployment will have an even greater impact on the size of the labor force than it would have on the size of the population. A larger number of emigrants would be expected to be of working age and either working or seeking work at the time of departure than the remaining population in Puerto Rico.

This chapter will consist of an analysis of the effect of emigration on the size and quality of the Puerto Rican labor force during the two decades of emigration. This chapter will consider these questions: What was the size of the labor force in the migration stream? What were the skill level and occupational and educational characteristics of the migrants? What effect did emigration have on the skill level and size of the labor force? What effect did emigration have on the unemployment problem in Puerto Rico? The answers to these questions will determine whether emigration was a positive or a negative factor in improving the quality of the Puerto Rican labor force and, in turn, whether this had a favorable effect on the growth of output and productivity.

The previous chapter on the effect of emigration on the population structure provides a clue to the type of emigration that occurred. The large majority of migrants were in the reproductive age bracket 15–44, which is also the most economically productive age period. Thus, it is to be expected from the impact on population that the migration stream is likely to have a greater number of migrants in the labor force than the proportion of labor force members in the Puerto Rican population. The effect would be a significant decrease in the size of the expected labor force in Puerto Rico during the period of emigration. Moreover, the future growth of the labor force will be reduced: there will be a smaller number of new labor force entrants fifteen to twenty years from now because of the reduction of births in Puerto Rico.

The migration hypothesis, advanced in the theoretical discussion, asserted that the occupational earnings differentials would stimulate the movement of a larger proportion of unskilled to skilled laborers than the existing ratio in the economy after a minimum income per capita is attained. If this proposition is valid, then the emigration will have a positive effect on improving the quality of the labor force by raising the ratio of skilled to unskilled workers. Thus, the a priori expectations are that emigration will have a significant effect on reducing the size and improving the quality of the labor force.

Puerto Rican Labor Force

Size of the Labor Force

Although the Puerto Rican economy experienced rapid growth of capital investment and total output of goods and services during the past twenty years, the size of the labor force did not grow appreciably. In 1940 the labor force contained 602,000 workers; in the next decade it increased to 713,000 workers, but declined thereafter to 625,000 in 1960. The sharp reduction of net emigration in the last three years, 1960–1963, was a major factor stimulating a sharp increase in the labor force. In 1963 the labor force was 670,000 workers.

One of the major factors determining the size of the economy's labor force is the demand for labor. When the demand for labor is high and the economy is experiencing shortages of labor, it is not unusual for new entrants into the labor force, particularly women and younger and older members of the population, to increase the size of the labor force. Conversely, when unemployment is high and the difficulty of securing employment is discouraging to labor force members, the size of the labor force may decrease as the unemployed members drop out. In addition, if the alternative of emigration is available to the unemployed workers, the lack of employment opportunities may be a factor stimulating the size of the migration stream.

Employment

In Puerto Rico, a failure to generate sufficient employment and the alternative opportunity to emigrate were the major factors contributing to the decrease in the size of the labor force during the 1950's. Employment in Puerto Rico, as seen in Table 4.1, did

TABLE 4.1

LABOR FORCE, EMPLOYMENT, AND UNEMPLOYMENT IN PUERTO RICO

	1940	1950	1960	1961	1962
Labor Force	602,000	686,000	625,000	639,000	670,000
Employment	536,000	596,000	542,000	564,000	585,000
Agriculture	230,000	216,000	125,000	134,000	139,000
Manufacturing	56,000	55,000	81,000	84,000	91,000
Commerce	54,000	90,000	97,000	94,000	100,000
Government	19,000	45,000	62,000	67,000	67,000
Other	177,000	190,000	177,000	185,000	188,000
Unemployment	66,000	88,000	83,000	75,000	84,000
Percentage of Unemployment	11	13	13	12	13

Source: Commonwealth of Puerto Rico, Office of the Governor, Puerto Rico Planning Board, Bureau of Economic and Social Planning, Selected Indices of Social and Economic Progress, Fiscal Years 1939–1940, 1946–1962 (San Juan, Commonwealth of Puerto Rico, 1962), pp. 3–4.

not grow significantly during the rapid stage of economic growth. Between 1940 and 1960 employment rose only 6,000 from 536,000 to 542,000. The population was available for an expanding labor force, but apparently employment was unavailable to stimulate the growth of the labor force. Even more alarming was the sharp decrease in employment from a peak of 596,000 jobs in 1950 to its low level of 542,000 in 1960. The major factor responsible for the decrease in employment was the sharp drop in agricultural employment during the 1950–1960 period. In 1940, agricultural employment was 230,000, the largest employment sector in the economy, and it decreased to 125,000 in 1960. This significant decrease offset the increases in nonagricultural employment. The changes in the labor force, employment by sector, and unemployment are presented in Table 4.1 for selected years.

It is interesting to note that significant increases in capital investment occurred throughout the two decades. (See tables in Chapter 6.) Gross fixed domestic investment in Puerto Rico rose from 23 million dollars in 1940 to 433 million dollars in 1962.[1] At the same time, nonagricultural employment increased by 121,000 and manufacturing employment increased by 35,000. Assuming a large percentage of capital investment allocated to the manufacturing sector of the economy, the employment generation in this sector was not very significant in relation to the growth of population and the decreases in agricultural employment. In short, the increase of manufacturing employment was not able to absorb the displaced agricultural workers, even though capital stock and output of the manufacturing sector grew rapidly. (See Chapter 6.) The lack of employment generation in the manufacturing sector was probably due, in part, to laborsaving capital investment.

The migration stream contained significant numbers of labor force members. Out of a total 617,000 migrants in the United States in 1960, 297,000 or 48 per cent were classified as labor force members.[2] Thus, the lack of sufficient employment generation and the large-scale emigration of Puerto Rican workers to the United States caused a sharp decrease during the decade of the 1950's and was responsible for the absence of change in the size of the labor force during the 1940–1960 period.

Labor Force Participation Rates

A comparison of the different labor force participation rates in Table 4.2 reveals that the migrant population had a significantly greater rate than the Puerto Rican population. Lines 6 and 10 are calculations of the expected labor force participation rates of

[1] Commonwealth of Puerto Rico, Office of the Governor, Puerto Rico Planning Board, Bureau of Economic and Social Planning, *Selected Indices of Social and Economic Progress, Fiscal Years 1939–40, 1946–62* (San Juan, Commonwealth of Puerto Rico, 1962).

[2] United States Department of Commerce, Bureau of the Census, *Census of Population: 1960, Puerto Ricans in the United States*, Special Final Report, PC(2)-ID (Washington, D. C.: United States Government Printing Office, 1963).

TABLE 4.2
MIGRANT AND PUERTO RICAN LABOR FORCE PARTICIPATION RATES
1930–1960
(*Percentages*)

	Total Population	Population 14+
Actual 1930 Rate for Puerto Rico	32.2	53.3
Actual 1940 Rate for Puerto Rico	32.2	52.1
Actual 1950 Rate for Puerto Rico	27.0	45.9
Actual 1950 Rate for Migrants	40.7	58.2
*Actual 1950 Rate for Migrants and Children	33.1	56.6
Expected Rate for Puerto Rico 1950 (lines 3 and 5)	32.3	53.4
Actual 1960 Rate for Puerto Rico	25.3	42.2
Actual 1960 Rate for Migrants	48.0	58.3
*Actual 1960 Rate for Migrants and Children	36.4	57.8
Expected Rate for Puerto Rico 1960 (lines 7 and 9)	31.2	46.4

* Migrants refers to people residing in the United States born in Puerto Rico. Children refers to offspring of migrants born in the United States.

Sources: U.S. Department of Commerce, Bureau of the Census, *Census of Population: 1950 and 1960, Puerto Ricans in the United States,* Special Final Report, PC(2)-1D, 1960, and PE 3D, 1950; *Characteristics of the Population,* Parts 51–54, *Territories and Possessions,* 1950; and *Puerto Rico, General and Detailed Characteristics: 1950 and 1960,* PC(1)53D and PC(1)53B (Washington, D. C.: United States Government Printing Office, 1963).

Puerto Rico, assuming that all migrants who are in the labor force in the United States would have remained in the Puerto Rican labor force. The expected rate without emigration in 1950 was 32.3 per cent of the total population, while the migrants residing in the United States had a rate of 40.7 per cent. In 1960 the difference in the labor force participation rate for the two populations widened; the Puerto Rican rate was 31.2 per cent, while the migrant rate was 48.0 per cent. The impact of the higher labor force participation rates among the migrants than in the Puerto Rican population caused a reduction in the rates that prevailed in Puerto Rico for the years 1950 and 1960. The rate declined from the expected 32.3 per cent to 27.0 per cent in 1950. The decrease was greater in 1960, from the expected rate of 31.2 per cent to the actual rate of 25.3 per cent.

Since the majority of the migrant population were between the ages of 15 and 44, it would be desirable to compare the labor force participation rates of the population 14 years and older to offset the heavy proportion of older and younger people in the Puerto Rican population. This standardization by age reveals whether any differential in the participation rate exists among a relatively homogeneous population with respect to age. It is expected that the migrant groups' differential compared to the Puerto Rican group would be reduced by this standardization. Table 4.2 provides the labor force participation rates of the population 14 years and over for the two groups. The migrant population still had a higher rate than the population on the island, although the differential was reduced. The expected rate in 1950 was 53.4 per cent, compared to the rate of the migrant population of 58.2 per cent; in 1960 the expected rate was 46.4 per cent for the Puerto Rican population and 58.3 per cent for the migrant group. The differences in the rates between 1950 and 1960 indicate that the emigration during the 1950's had an even greater proportion of labor force members than the migrants prior to 1950.

Labor force participation rate changes can result from changes in the age structure of the population and increased education, regardless of migration. Increased births and reduced deaths can stimulate a heavier proportion of young and old members of the population. An increased education also delays the age of entrance into the labor force. In order to evaluate whether and to what extent migration or these other factors accounted for the large decreases in the labor force participation rates, it is necessary to examine the rates for the total Puerto Rican population in the United States (which includes migrants' children) and the total Puerto Rican population on the island. This comparison tends to reduce the significance of changes resulting from age structure and increased education because similar changes take place in both population groups.

Table 4.2 also contains the labor force participation rates of the total Puerto Rican population in the United States. This rate was higher than the Puerto Rican rate, although the difference was lower than the other comparisons of the labor force participation rates. In 1950 the differential was almost negligible; the United States rate was 33.1 per cent while the Puerto Rican expected rate on the island was 32.3 per cent and the actual rate was 27.0 per cent. In 1960 the rate was higher for Puerto Ricans in the United States, 36.4 per cent, while the expected rate in Puerto Rico was 31.2 per cent and the actual rate was 25.3 per cent. This comparison indicates that the emigration was the basic determinant

TABLE 4.3

LAROR FORCE PARTICIPATION RATES OF THE MIGRANTS AND THE
POPULATION OF PUERTO RICO BY AGE AND SEX FOR SELECTED YEARS
1950 AND 1960
(*Percentages*)

Year	Male		Female	
1960	Migrants	Puerto Rico	Migrants	Puerto Rico
14+	79.0	65.7	36.0	20.0
14–19	39.0	29.0	23.0	0.9
20–24	91.0	77.0	46.0	32.0
25–34	91.0	86.0	39.0	29.0
35–44	91.0	93.0	45.0	25.0
45–64	81.0	81.0	33.0	18.0
65+	23.0	27.0	0.5	0.4
1950				
14+	76.0	70.7	39.0	21.3
14–24	65.0	51.0	40.0	22.0
25–44	86.0	84.0	44.0	25.0
45+	77.0	52.0	19.0	11.0

Source: United States Department of Commerce, Bureau of the Census, *Census of Population: 1950 and 1960, Puerto Rico* and *Census of Population: 1950 and 1960, Puerto Ricans in the United States* (Washington, D. C.: United States Government Printing Office, 1963).

of the decreases in the labor force participation rates in Puerto Rico.

Age-Sex Labor Force Participation Rates

A comparison of the labor force participation rates of the migrant population in the United States and the Puerto Rican population by age and sex are presented in Table 4.3. The data indicate that age and sex groups had significantly different participation rates. The 1950 data indicate that the female participation rates for the age groups from 14 to 24 years and 24 to 44 years were significantly higher for the migrants than for the remaining population on the island. The females of 45+ also had a higher labor force participation rate than their island counterparts but the difference was less than the other age groups. The male labor force participation rates by age for 1950 indicate that, although the migrants had a higher rate for every age grouping, the most significant difference occurred in the oldest age bracket, 45+, a direct contrast to the female participation rates by age. The labor force participation rates for males of 14+ were significantly higher for the migrant population than for the island population; but the female labor force participation rate difference was even greater between the migrants and the island population.

The 1960 labor force participation rates indicate that the migrants, both male and female, had higher rates than those on the island; but the difference between male participation rates increased, while the female participation rates decreased. This indicates that the recent migration contained a larger number of male than female labor force members compared to the pre-1950 migration. The Puerto Rican male participation rate for those over 14 years decreased from 70.7 in 1950 to 65.7 in 1960, while the rate for the migrants increased from 76.0 to 79.0. The female participation rate in Puerto Rico decreased slightly from 21.3 in 1950 to 20.0 in 1960.

The specific age-sex labor force participation rates indicate which groups dominated the migrant population. The most significant differences between participation rates of males in the two populations were in the age brackets 14 to 19 and 20 to 24; the rates were 39.0 for migrants and 29.0 for Puerto Rico, and 91.0 for migrants and 77.0 for Puerto Rico for the two age groups, respectively. Table 4.3 indicates that for the remaining age groups the male participation rates were quite similar.

The differences in the female participation rates by age indicate that the migrants had a significantly higher participation rate than the island population. The youngest age group — 14 to 19 — had the most significant differences in the female labor force participation rate; for the migrants the rate was 23.0 and for the island population it was only 0.9. In contrast to the male participation rates, the migrant female participation rates for all age groups was significantly higher than the island female participation rates.

In summary, the comparisons of age-sex labor force participation rates for the Puerto Rican migrants in the United States and the Puerto Rican population on the island indicate that the migrants had (1) significantly higher labor force participation rates than the island; (2) female labor participation rates were higher in every age group for both sexes than on the island; and (3) the bulk of labor force members who emigrated were in the age group 14 to 24 for both sexes and had significantly higher labor force participation rates compared to their island counterparts. Thus, the comparisons of all the combinations of segments of the migrant and the Puerto Rican populations clearly indicate that the migrants had a considerably higher labor force participation rate and emigration caused the rate on the island to fall significantly during the twenty-year period of emigration and rapid economic growth.

The changes in the labor force participation rates in Puerto Rico from 1930–1960 are presented in Table 4.2. The rate remained stable between 1930 and 1940 and began to decrease in the 1940–1950 period. The largest decrease was the decline of the male participation rate from 48.8 per cent to 41.3 per cent during the ten-year period, while the female participation rate decreased from 15.5 per cent to 12.6 per cent. In percentage terms, the female decrease exceeded the male decrease by 18.6 per cent to 15.6 per cent. The labor force participation rate continued to decline throughout the fifties but at a slower pace. Of particular interest, the female rate showed a negligible decrease in the 1950's. This circumstance is reflected in the absence of increases of the female rate of Puerto Ricans in the United States. In fact, it accounts for the decline in the Puerto Rican female labor force participation rate in the United States. In 1950 the female rate was 30.4 per cent and in 1960 it decreased to 29.9 per cent for the total Puerto Rican population; for the population of 14 years or over it decreased even more — from 41.0 per cent in 1950 to 36.3 per cent in 1960. In contrast, the male participation rate of the migrants increased significantly from 51.7 per cent in 1950 to 66.3 per cent in 1960 for the total population, and for the population of 14 years and over it increased only slightly: 79.4 per cent to 80.5 per cent in 1960. These figures support the finding that the migrant population contained a greater number of male workers than female in the later period, 1950–1960, than prior to 1950.

It is also quite possible that female migrants in the United States who were working in 1950 and/or during the 1950's but married during the same period of time would have dropped out of the labor force statistics in the 1960 census. It is possible that the female dropouts are related to the increased earnings of their husbands, which makes it no longer necessary for a household to have two sources of income. Although these reasons may have contributed to the decreased female participation rate, the fact that the rate decreased insignificantly in Puerto Rico indicates that a large part of the explanation of the declining rate was the absence of female workers in the migrant stream. Furthermore, additional evidence from the ramp survey[3] of migrants departing from Puerto Rico indicates that 91 per cent of the net migration of residents were male labor force members compared to 9 per cent female.

In summary, the major findings of the comparisons of labor force participation rates indicate that there was a considerably higher rate in the migrant population than on the island of Puerto Rico. This differential in the rates caused a significant decrease in the labor force participation rate in Puerto Rico for the period 1940–1960. The changes in male and female rates indicate that the migration prior to 1950 had a greater number of female workers than the migration of 1950–1960. In general, the large number of labor force members who emigrated support the conclusion that the migration was primarily economically motivated.

Dependency Ratio of the Puerto Rican Population

The incidence of a greater labor force participation rate among the migrant population should have caused a significant reduction in the ratio of productive to nonproductive members of the population. The declining labor force participation rate, depicted in Table 4.3, indicates an increased dependency of the population. One of the reasons for the greater number of dependents is the increased longevity, thus increasing the proportion of elderly people in the population. The declining birth rate observed in Puerto Rico during this period reduced the proportion of young dependents in the population. The sharper decline in the 1940's indicates that the early migration contained many more single workers than the 1950's, which contained more labor force members but also a considerably larger number of dependent people. In short, the difference stems from the change from a movement of individuals to a family migration. It is possible that once the individual worker secured a job and saved enough money, he would then send for his family who arrived in the decade of the 1950's. This conforms to a similar pattern observed in other migrant groups who came to the United States in earlier periods.

Since the bulk of the postwar migration occurred in the 1950–

---

[3] Commonwealth of Puerto Rico, Department of Labor, Bureau of Labor Statistics, 1957–1962, *Characteristics of Passengers Who Traveled by Air between Puerto Rico and the United States.* The sample survey of passengers entering and leaving Puerto Rico was initiated by the Puerto Rican government in 1957 in order to obtain information on the characteristics of the passengers.

1960 period, it would be expected that the dependency proportion would have been even higher in 1960. However, the dependency ratio did not increase as rapidly as expected because of the family-type migration during the 1950's, which removed a sizable number of the dependent population. If the ratio had been the same, that is, an equal number of productive to nonproductive people in the migration stream as in the population, then the dependency proportion would not have been altered.

Nevertheless, the emigration stream did contain more productive members than the population, thus affecting the dependency proportion of the Puerto Rican population. This increased dependency proportion neither implies nor reflects an undesirable state of economic conditions: often it is a sign of affluence rather than poverty. The crucial problem is whether the level of living increased despite the decrease in the size of the labor force. In the case of Puerto Rico, income per worker and income per capita both increased significantly, despite a smaller labor force. This reflects a very significant increase in output per worker, sufficient to offset the decrease in the productive proportion of the population and allow income per capita to increase. (See Chapter 6.)

On practical grounds, the use of the labor force as an indicator of the productive population is misleading. In reality, it is only the employed workers who are productive members of the population, and large-scale unemployment will increase the dependency ratio considerably. Potential and actual productive populations are totally different in an economy that experiences persistent and large-scale unemployment. Defining the actual productive proportion of a population as the percentage of the employed labor force out of the total population provides a better indication of the changes in the dependency ratio in Puerto Rico. In 1940, the rate of productive (employed) members of the total population was 27 per cent; in 1950 it decreased to 25 per cent; and in 1960 it decreased slightly to 24 per cent. Taking the employed out of the total population fourteen and over, it was 44 per cent in 1940, 43 per cent in 1950, and it decreased to 39 per cent in 1960. The proportion of productive workers decreased by only 11.4 per cent in the two decades, in contrast to a 20 per cent decrease of the labor force participation rates. The larger decrease in the labor force rate indicates that a significant number of migrants were either unemployed or were replaced by new entrants into the labor force or other unemployed members in the Puerto Rican economy. A third possibility is that the workers were replaced by capital-intensive, laborsaving machinery. In part, this hints at the composition of the migrant stream with regard to skill and occupation of the migrants. Unskilled occupations are often most easily replaced with either machinery or other workers than are skilled occupations.

Occupational Distribution of the Puerto Rican Labor Force

The occupational distribution of the labor force provides an indication of its skill level. The changes in the distribution of occupations indicate the changes in the quality of the labor force. The return movement of workers from the United States back to Puerto Rico has been a recent phenomenon and of a smaller magnitude than the outflow of labor in all occupations, with the exception of professional and managerial occupations in 1960 and 1961. Therefore, the existing improvement in the quality of the labor force during the past two decades has been primarily a direct result of large-scale government expenditures in the area of formal public education and vocational training. Large-scale capital investments often increase the demand for skilled labor; thus they may have provided incentives for the better use of the new educational facilities.

The changes in the occupational distribution of the Puerto Rican labor force over the two decades, 1940–1960, are presented in Table 4.4. The occupational distribution changed significantly during the period 1940–1960. An upgrading of the labor force occurred and, although the trend toward more skilled and industrial occupations is to be expected as the economy grows and industrializes, the rapid speed of these changes within a short period of time merits attention.[4] These rapid changes in the occupational structure of the labor force are attributed to three major factors: (1) the rapid growth of the industrial sector; (2) heavy investment in public and vocational education; and (3) large-scale emigration. The last

[4] Stanley Lebergott, *Manpower in Economic Growth: the American Record since 1800* (New York: McGraw-Hill Book Co., 1964), p. 512. The remarkable change in the number of people engaged in farm occupations is more striking when contrasted to the length of time it took for the decline in farm employment in the United States. Lebergott's statistics for farm employment in the United States show that in 1900 there were 11,680,000 workers employed in agriculture and in 1960 it had decreased to 5,970,000, or a decrease in absolute numbers of 50 per cent. In a short span of less than twenty years the number of people engaged in agriculture in Puerto Rico decreased from 240,000 to approximately 120,000, or a 50 per cent decrease.

TABLE 4.4
OCCUPATIONAL DISTRIBUTION OF THE EMPLOYED PUERTO RICAN LABOR FORCE, 1940, 1950, 1960

Occupations	1940		1950		Change 1940–1950		1960		Change 1950–1960		Change 1940–1960	
	Number	Per Cent	Number	Per Cent	Number	Per Cent	Number	Per Cent	Number	Per Cent	Number	Per Cent
Professional and Technical	15,297	3.0	26,913	4.8	11,617	76	43,116	7.8	16,203	60	27,820	182
Farmers and Farm Mgrs.	47,761	9.3	36,230	6.5	—11,531	—24	17,852	3.2	—18,738	—51	—29,909	—63
Mgrs., Owners and Officials	24,380	4.8	33,161	5.9	8,781	36	40,472	7.3	7,313	22	16,049	66
Clerical	19,539	3.8	27,485	4.9	7,946	41	42,768	7.8	15,283	56	23,229	119
Sales	22,000	4.3	29,179	5.2	7,179	33	34,888	6.3	5,709	20	12,888	59
Craftsmen and Foremen	27,550	5.4	42,187	7.5	14,637	53	60,748	11.0	18,561	41	33,198	121
Operatives	91,651	17.9	92,642	16.4	993	1	99,196	18.0	6,553	7	7,545	8
Domestic	39,335	7.7	32,649	5.8	— 6,686	—17	18,988	3.4	—13,661	—42	—20,346	—52
All Other Service	18,507	3.6	29,858	5.3	11,352	61	42,508	7.7	12,649	42	24,001	130
Farm Laborers	178,304	34.8	173,219	30.9	— 5,085	— 3	109,492	19.8	—63,727	—37	—68,812	—39
Laborers	26,274	5.1	31,160	5.6	4,886	19	34,244	6.2	3,084	10	7,970	30
TOTAL	512,214		560,271				551,688					

Sources: United States Department of Commerce, Bureau of the Census, *Census of Population: 1950 and 1960, Puerto Rico, General and Detailed Characteristics,* PC(1)53D, PC(1)53B (Washington, D. C.: United States Government Printing Office, 1963) and Commonwealth of Puerto Rico, Planning Board, Comparative Statistics of the San Juan Metropolitan Area (San Juan, Commonwealth of Puerto Rico, 1961), pp. 30–31.

factor, although not directly contributing to the increased numbers of skilled personnel, did affect the percentage distribution of the occupational structure. The two most significant changes were the rapid increases in the skilled occupational classifications of professional and technical manpower and craftsmen and foremen and the sharp decrease in the number of workers engaged in farm occupations as either laborers or farmers.

Changes in the Quality of the Labor Force

The prevention of a skilled labor bottleneck and the external economies derived from possessing a skilled, educated, and mobile labor force are extremely important to the successful development of an industrial economy. The attraction of industries and capital investment often is determined by whether a skilled and productive labor force is available. The growth of skilled professional and technical manpower in a short span of twenty years in Puerto Rico was probably an instrumental factor in attracting large amounts of new, modern, and complex industries from the United States. The growth of professional, technical, managerial, and craftsmen occupations can be easily observed in Table 4.4. The professional and technical occupations experienced the largest increase: 181.9 per cent in two decades. The actual number practically trebled in the twenty-year period. The percentage of the labor force employed in this occupational group rose from a low of 3.0 per cent to 7.8 per cent.

Another highly skilled occupation — craftsmen and foremen — also increased its numbers considerably from 27,550 in 1940 to 60,-748 in 1960. This increase represents a jump of 120.5 per cent, raising the percentage of this occupation of the total employed labor force from 5.4 per cent in 1940 to 11.0 per cent in 1960. In light of the longer period required to obtain the training to enter these highly skilled occupations, the rapid increases that were achieved are even more striking.

The growth of the tertiary service industries and the expansion of the government sector led to a rapid increase in the number of people engaged in service occupations, which increased 129.6 per cent, raising the percentage of the labor force engaged in this occupation to 7.7 per cent in 1960.

The occupational classification of managers and officials did not increase as significantly as some of the other occupation groups, rising only 66 per cent and increasing its percentage of the employed labor force from 4.7 per cent in 1940 to 7.3 per cent in 1960. The lack of rapid growth of this occupational classification may reflect the uncertainty, for young men emerging from a low socioeconomic background, of obtaining employment as a manager and/or official. Often in a traditional economic environment a son or relative will have a considerably better chance to obtain employment in this occupation. The observed difficulty of obtaining employment in these important decision-making positions may have stimulated many more young people to obtain specific skills. In this way they seek entrance into occupations where traditionally merit, not connections, is the avenue for stable, respectable employment.

On the other hand, the smaller increases in the number and percentage of the managerial classification may not reflect the improvement in the quality within this group. It is quite easy in a relatively backward industrial sector for many people with limited amounts of capital to set up small job shops and retail outlets. These people will no doubt be registered in the surveys and census reports as managers and officials. Neglecting entrepreneurial talent, the educational and skill level of these managers is often not sufficient to enable them to succeed in a highly industrialized, competitive economic environment. Thus, they are not equivalents of the professionally trained and educated manager. The numbers engaged in this managerial occupation may not have increased rapidly but the quality of the group probably did.

The rapid growth of the economy and the increased purchasing power derived from the rising income per capita stimulated a rapid increase in the number of people engaged in the clerical and sales classifications. The number increased 118.8 per cent in the twenty-year period for clerical workers and 58.6 per cent for sales workers. The growth of the government sector was responsible for part of the rapid increase in the workers in the clerical occupations.

One of the most unusual features of the industrial occupational distribution of the labor force is the total absence of any change in the operatives classification. The very small increase of 8.2 per cent is even more striking considering the rapid growth of output in the manufacturing sector.[5] Apparently there has been a replacement of operatives with laborsaving machinery in this sector. The proportion of operatives in the employed labor force remained

[5] *Selected Indices, op. cit.*, pp. 2–3. Manufacturing output increased in dollar terms from $27 million in 1940 to $381 million in 1962 in Puerto Rico.

remarkably stable: 17.8 per cent in 1940 and 17.9 per cent in 1960. The total increase of the number of operatives in the 1940–1950 period was an unusually small 993 workers, or a 1.1 per cent increase.

The other unskilled occupations did not show any appreciable increases, especially the laborers. With the rapid growth of the construction industry and the increases in trade and the movement of goods and services, it was expected that there would be a substantial increase in the number of workers in this category. Contrary to this expectation, the number of laborers increased only 30.8 per cent. During the rapid growth period, 1950–1960, the number of laborers increased by 3,084, or 9.9 per cent. Again, this provides some evidence indicating the substitution of laborsaving machinery for unskilled laborers.

With rapid industrial growth, it is expected that the number of people engaged in the agricultural occupations would decline relative to the industrial occupations. The decrease was even greater than expected — that is, the agricultural occupations experienced a significant decrease in the absolute numbers engaged in these occupations. The greatest decline, 38.6 per cent, occurred among farm laborers and foremen. This decline is even more significant in terms of percentages of the employed labor force, from a high 34.8 per cent in 1940 to a low of 19.8 per cent in 1960.

The occupational classification of farmers and farm managers decreased even more than farm laborers in percentage terms, 62.2 per cent, causing a sharp decrease in the percentage of the employed labor force in this classification from 9.3 per cent in 1940 to 3.2 per cent in 1960. The reduction in farmers and farm managers reflects the declining importance of the agricultural sector, but even more important it reflects the increase in the size of farm holdings in Puerto Rico.[6] The number of farmers decreased from 47,761 in 1940 to 18,378 in 1960. No doubt that the increased size of farms and the introduction of capital equipment to replace labor-intensive methods contributed to the growth of output and productivity in the agricultural sector.[7]

The upgrading of the labor force between the two decades can easily be observed by examining the columns indicating the percentage of each occupation in the total employed labor force. The

[6] The changes in labor supply, productivity, and output in the agricultural sector are presented in a later chapter.

[7] Agricultural output increased in dollar terms from $71 million in 1940 to $208 million in 1962.

rapid decreases in the unskilled occupations and the rapid increases in the skilled occupations have resulted in a vastly improved labor force in the short period of twenty years. The transformation from a traditional agricultural economy to a rapidly expanding industrial economy is reflected in the significant changes in the occupational distribution of the labor force. The skilled occupations of professional, managerial, and craftsmen amounted to only 12.9 per cent of the employed labor force in 1940, compared to 38.9 per cent for the unskilled occupations of farm laborers and laborers. The 1960 percentages showed a tremendous reversal; the skilled occupations comprised 26.2 per cent of the labor force, while the unskilled percentage had decreased to 26 per cent. This reflects the significant change in the ratio of skilled to unskilled workers in the Puerto Rican economy.

Effects of Emigration on the Size and Quality of the Puerto Rican Labor Force

The United States Population Census provides a special report of Puerto Ricans residing in the United States for 1950 and 1960.[8] Although a better method of estimating the number and occupations of labor force members among the migrant population would be a complete sample survey of the status of the migrants at their time of departure, unfortunately this is not available for the entire period of emigration. Nevertheless, the data from the census reports are a good approximation of the information needed to analyze the effect of emigration on the size and quality of the labor force.

Under the assumption that all Puerto Ricans in the United States who are in the labor force would have remained in the labor force if residing in Puerto Rico, we can arrive at an estimate of the size of the labor force if emigration had not occurred. The major difficulty with the assumption is the distinct possibility that many of the Puerto Ricans in the United States labor force may have entered the labor force because of the existence of job availabilities, while they may not have entered the Puerto Rican labor force because of the lack of jobs. In any event, the return of the Puerto Rican emigrants, or the absence of emigration, would have added 296,665

---

[8] United States Department of Commerce, Bureau of the Census, *Census of the Population: 1950, 1960*, Special Report, P-E No. 3D; *Puerto Ricans in the Continental United States, 1950*, Vol. IV, Part 3 (Washington D. C.: U.S. Government Printing Office, 1953); *Puerto Ricans in the United States, op. cit.*

Puerto Ricans who were born in Puerto Rico and a grand total of 325,000 Puerto Ricans, including the children of Puerto Ricans born in the United States, to the existing labor force in Puerto Rico. The sum of both labor force groups would total 961,000 labor force members on the island in 1960, or a 50 per cent increase in the size of the labor force.

A conservative estimate of the Puerto Rican labor force without emigration for 1970 brings the size of the labor force to 1,190,000 workers,[9] or nearly twice (88 per cent) as many available workers as were on the island of Puerto Rico in 1960. The combined effect of the children of the migrants and the children on the island would swell the size of the new entrants into the labor force in 1970. It is quite apparent that had there been no emigration the Puerto Rican economy would have had to supply a great many more jobs than it has generated in the past two decades. This leads to the important question of what would have been the effect on unemployment if either emigration had not occurred or if all the migrants should return to Puerto Rico. The size of the return flow has increased significantly in the last five years and the net outflow is quite small compared to that of the decade of the 1950's. If the reverse movement continues to grow and large-scale immigration back to the island occurs, the unemployment problem on the island will reach alarming proportions.

Unemployment

The inability of the Puerto Rican economy to reduce the rate of unemployment during the twenty years of rapid economic growth and capital formation raises serious implications about the amount of unemployment that would have prevailed in the absence of emigration or if emigration was of insignificant size. It should be pointed out that although the rate of unemployment did not decrease, undoubtedly the growth of the economy and emigration reduced the amount of unmeasured disguised unemployment and underemployment in the agricultural and industrial sectors of the economy. The measured rate of unemployment in Puerto Rico averaged approximately 13 per cent throughout the 1940–1960

---

[9] This estimate was calculated by combining the total number of new entrants into the labor force, those reaching fourteen years or more by 1970, taking a 40 per cent of this total as the labor force participation rate, and adding the result to the labor force of 1970 after deducting dropouts from retirement.

period. The range was 11 per cent in 1940 and 16 per cent in 1952.

It is difficult to estimate the amount of unemployment had there been no emigration because the other variables cannot realistically be held constant. Specifically, what effect would the increased size of the labor force have had on the type and amount of capital investment in Puerto Rico? It is conceivable that the rise in real wages (if it was due to emigration) stimulated laborsaving, capital-intensive investment and that, if real wages had not risen, the capital invested would have been directed into labor-intensive industries and have generated greater employment. This type of investment may have reduced the unemployment, but it also would have resulted in lower output per worker, compared to higher capital-labor ratios and higher output per worker with capital-intensive investment.

On the other hand, real wages in Puerto Rico remained significantly below the wages in the United States (see Chapter 5), and thus it would have been profitable for firms to invest in labor-intensive industries to take advantage of the lower labor costs in Puerto Rico. Another factor to be considered is that, even with excess supplies of labor (high unemployment), wage rates may not adjust rapidly in a downward direction, especially where unions resist wage rate reductions and/or skilled occupations are in short supply. Thus, for those industries that are unionized or have a demand for skilled labor, wages will probably not decrease sufficiently, and most likely will increase more rapidly, stimulating the switch to capital-intensive rather than labor-intensive methods.

On the basis of the above conditions and the fact that the Puerto Rican government and industrialists have made a supreme effort in attracting foreign and domestic capital investment, one can determine the maximum unemployment on the island assuming that additional capital was not available and that the type of capital investment would not have been altered significantly.

Under this assumption, the additional 325,000 workers in the labor force would have either pushed other workers out of their jobs or would not have found employment themselves. In either case, an additional 325,000 unemployed workers would be in the Puerto Rican economy. This would increase the unemployment figure to approximately 407,000, or 42.8 per cent of the labor force. This figure needs to be modified because in reality many of these additional workers would have returned to the rural agricultural sector and increased the ranks of the disguised unemployed but would not be registered in the measured unemployment. Obviously, negative effects on the agricultural sector would result if the emigrants returned to the farms. For example, agricultural employment in 1960 was 125,000 workers, and with the return flow of migrants back to Puerto Rico, thereby decreasing net emigration, the employment in this sector rose to 139,000 in 1962. In addition, other workers would find employment at lower occupational skill jobs than they had previously, resulting in greater amounts of underemployment for a segment of the labor force.

Last of all, large numbers of these workers would find employment in service occupations or retail or wholesale trading. This merely represents another form of disguised unemployment since each reduces the sales of the others; a smaller number of salesmen could sell as much as the excessive number in the marketplace. All these different types of employment would not contribute to the growth of total output of goods and services, and in many cases would reduce it. But the measured rate of unemployment would be reduced, easing the social pressures that may have led to demands and actions to change the social, political, and economic structure of the island.

A Revised Estimate of Unemployment

This maximum unemployment rate, however, is somewhat unrealistic. Let us assume that 10 per cent of the Puerto Rican labor force members in the United States drop out because of the lack of jobs in Puerto Rico, another 20 per cent return to the agricultural sector, another 20 per cent find employment in lower skilled occupations and/or as disguised unemployed retailers, and 10 per cent are employed following the addition of fixed capital investment of $110,442,000.[10] This still leaves 40 per cent of the 325,000 additional labor force members unemployed, or a total of 130,000 workers. Adding this amount to the 82,000 presently unemployed would result in 212,000 workers unemployed, or 22.4 per cent of the labor force. This significant increase could cause serious political, social, and economic problems on the island and definitely help retard the rate of future economic growth and lower the achieved increases

[10] This capital invested figure was derived by assuming the maintenance of the existing capital-labor ratio in 1960, which in terms of gross fixed domestic investment was $3,389 per worker, and multiplying by 32,500 workers to obtain $110,442,000 additional gross fixed domestic capital needed.

in income per capita as well as the standard of living on the island of Puerto Rico.

An estimate of the minimum lower limit of unemployment would require the assumption that enough capital investment took place to employ the additional workers in the same proportion as occurred with emigration. In other words, the rate of unemployment would remain the same but the actual numbers of unemployed would increase. A modification of this estimate would be to calculate first the specific unemployment rates by occupation and then the effect of unemployment with the net additions of the unemployed in each occupation if emigration had not occurred. Since the migrants were generally more unskilled than the labor force in Puerto Rico, the unemployment rate and number should be greater than merely maintaining the same rate of unemployment. The rate of unemployment by occupation is only available for the experienced civilian labor force. This rate is considerably below the actual prevailing rate of unemployment; new workers have significantly higher unemployment rates than experienced workers. It was necessary to adjust the unemployment of the experienced labor force to the total unemployment of the entire labor force. A weight of 2.56 was calculated and multiplied by the civilian rate of unemployment to make the occupational unemployment equivalent to the unemployment rate of the total labor force. The result of the calculation gives a total unemployment of 110,000, or approximately 14 per cent unemployment rate. This percentage and number are underestimated, since the occupations not reported are not included in the estimate.

The basic problem with the lower limit estimate is the unrealistic amounts of capital needed to employ the additional workers. The amount of increase in gross domestic fixed investment needed to employ the additional 325,000 workers in order to maintain the capital-labor ratio and output per worker ratio would have been an additional $1,101,425,000, or 55 per cent of gross commonwealth product (GCP) in 1960. To maintain the 1950 capital-labor ratio and output per worker ratio would have required $367,142,000 additional capital, or 48 per cent of GCP in 1950; and for 1940 ratios to be maintained, it would have required another $124,150,000, or 43 per cent of GCP in 1940. Given all the efforts to raise additional capital by the government and the private entrepreneurs in Puerto Rico, it is extremely doubtful whether the economy could have obtained any significant amount of additional capital. In view of the magnitudes of capital needed, it seems as if the amount of unemployment would probably fall between the modified upper limit of 22 per cent and the maximum upper limit of 43 per cent, probably closer to the lower figure. In any event, a significant amount of unemployment would have emerged on the island if emigration had not taken place. The rate of unemployment in the future may increase rapidly if the emigration ceases or if immigration occurs. The increased size of the new entrants into the labor force in the coming years will itself demand that the economy provide thousands of new jobs or else face the problem of rising unemployment, especially among better educated youths.

Effect of Emigration on the Quality of the Labor Force

Aside from the withdrawal of large numbers of workers in all occupational classifications, emigration had a definite impact on the skill composition of the remaining labor force. If the skill mix in the migration population was different from the mix in the Puerto Rican population, then a change in the skill distribution of the labor force would occur. Before proceeding to examine the impact of emigration on the occupational distribution of the labor force, it is first necessary to examine the characteristics of the migrants.

The occupations, skill, and educational levels of the migrants can have a profound impact on the quality of the remaining labor force. The excitement caused by the departure of a group of leading British scientists to the United States illustrates the concern given to the depletion of valuable human resources. The problem becomes more serious in countries where a severe shortage of skilled personnel exists. The loss of valuable human resources can have considerable negative effects on entrepreneurship, savings, labor productivity, attraction of capital, innovation, imitation, and invention. Thus, it is of the utmost importance to possess information on the characteristics of the migrants in order to assess the effect of their departure on the economy.

For the present analysis, the census report on Puerto Ricans residing in the United States provides sufficient information on the educational and occupational characteristics of the migrants to assess the impact on the distribution of the labor force in Puerto Rico, under the assumption that emigration had not occurred. The major weakness of utilizing the census material on the occupational classifications of the migrants and then placing these occupations in the distribution of the Puerto Rican labor force is that the occupations of the migrants may have been upgraded during their stay in the United States, but would have remained the same had they remained in Puerto Rico. It is also possible that discrimination against Puerto Ricans in the United States may have prevented upgrading that would have occurred in Puerto Rico. Another problem with the data is that the industrial structure of the United States requires the Puerto Ricans to change their occupations without changing their skill levels. In other words, farm laborers are not needed in the United States, and Puerto Rican farm laborers enter other unskilled occupations such as service workers, laborers, and operatives. There is ease of occupational transferability among homogeneous skill-grouped occupations. This obviously does not change the skill level, but it does change the percentages engaged in each occupational classification. Consolidating occupational classifications by skill levels avoids the problem of occupational transfers.

Quality of the Migrant Labor Force

The occupational distribution of migrants (Puerto Ricans born in Puerto Rico but residing in the United States) is presented in Table 4.5, column *B*. The greatest number of migrants was engaged in the operatives classification — 125,502 out of 242,229 workers, or over 50 per cent. Many migrants who were farmers and farm laborers in Puerto Rico would have been working in this occupation in the United States. For evidence supporting this transfer, the ramp survey of occupations of migrants at the time of departure for 1957–1961 reveals that the largest number of migrants was farm laborers, over 35 per cent of the total migrant population and over 62 per cent of the working migrant population.

The migration stream drained the economy of 6,718 professional and technical workers, 6,309 managers and officials, and 19,453 craftsmen and foremen. This represents a reduction of 15.8 per cent of the professional workers, 15.7 per cent of the managerial group, and 31.0 per cent of the craftsmen and foremen who were engaged in these occupations in Puerto Rico. It is impossible to assess from the census material the degree of skills among the different suboccupations under the broad classifications used in the census.

In Table 4.5, column *C* presents the total number of Puerto Ricans in the United States (including Puerto Ricans born in Puerto Rico and their children born in the United States) engaged in spe-

TABLE 4.5

OCCUPATIONAL DISTRIBUTION OF THE MIGRANT AND
PUERTO RICAN POPULATION 1960

Occupations	Puerto Rico A	Migrants B	Migrants and Children Born in the United States C	Total Columns A and B D	Total Columns A, B, and C E
Professional and Technical	43,116	6,178	8,691	49,834	51,807
Farmers and Farm Managers	17,852	197	227	18,049	18,079
Owners, Managers, and Officials	40,472	6,309	7,178	46,781	47,650
Clerical and Sales	77,656	26,425	33,762	104,081	111,418
Craftsmen and Foremen	60,748	19,453	22,297	80,201	83,045
Operatives	99,196	125,502	131,823	224,698	231,019
Domestic Service	18,988	909	1,121	19,897	20,109
All Other Service	42,568	36,848	39,401	79,356	81,969
Farm Laborers	109,492	5,732	5,878	115,224	115,370
Laborers	34,244	15,436	16,681	49,680	50,925
TOTAL	544,302	242,229	267,059	786,531	811,361

The occupational distribution is for the employed labor force; unreported occupations have been omitted.

Sources: United States Department of Commerce, Bureau of the Census, *Census of the Population: 1960, Puerto Rico, General Characteristics,* PC(1)53B (data for column 1) and *Census of Population: 1960, Puerto Ricans in the United States,* Special Final Report, PC(2)-1D (data for columns 2 and 3) (Washington, D. C.: United States Government Printing Office, 1961 and 1963).

cific occupations. The occupational classifications of those of Puerto Rican parentage indicate an upgrading of the occupations compared to their parents. This conforms to the traditional pattern of greater economic and social mobility among the children of the migrant groups. Increased educational facilities and greater motivation among the children have allowed a larger number to enter professional, craftsmen, and clerical occupations, causing an even greater drain from the skilled groups in the Puerto Rican labor force. This assumes that the children of the migrants would have

TABLE 4.6

OCCUPATIONAL DISTRIBUTION OF THE MIGRANT AND PUERTO RICAN
LABOR FORCE FOR SELECTED YEARS 1950 AND 1960
(*Percentages*)

Occupations	Puerto Rico 1960	Migrants 1960	Columns 1 and 2 Combined	Puerto Rico 1950	Migrants 1950
Professional and Technical	7.9	2.8	6.4	4.8	4.3
Farmers and Farm Managers	3.3	0.1	2.3	6.5	0.1
Owners, Managers, and Officials	7.4	2.6	6.0	5.9	3.8
Clerical and Sales	14.3	10.9	12.1	5.1	8.4
Craftsmen and Foremen	11.2	8.0	10.3	7.5	7.5
Operatives	18.2	51.8	28.8	16.5	48.4
Domestic Service	3.5	0.4	2.5	5.8	1.0
All Other Service	7.8	15.2	10.2	5.3	18.6
Farm Laborers	20.1	2.4	14.8	30.9	5.0
Laborers	6.3	6.4	6.4	5.6	5.0

Sources: Data taken from Table 4.5.

had the opportunity to continue school in Puerto Rico without interfering with higher educational opportunities of other children because of the limited educational resources in Puerto Rico.

Adding the occupational breakdown of Puerto Ricans in the United States to the figures in Puerto Rico gives an estimate of the occupational distribution of the Puerto Rican labor force if migration had not occurred. Table 4.5, columns *D* and *E*, gives the distributions with the migrants and the migrants and their children, respectively. The actual numbers are translated into percentage terms for each occupation and provide a more meaningful comparison of the changes in the different occupations in the labor force as a result of the absence of emigration. The results appear in Table 4.6. The heavy proportion of unskilled occupations in the migration stream in relation to the Puerto Rican labor force caused a decrease in the percentages of skilled occupations and an increase in the unskilled occupations. The most significant change was the sharp increase in the percentage of the operatives, rising from 18.2 per cent to 28.8 per cent. As pointed out previously, many of these operatives were laborers in Puerto Rico. It is possible that they never would have been operatives in Puerto Rico unless the demand for operatives had increased significantly.

All the skilled occupations decreased in percentage terms, professionals falling from 7.9 per cent to 6.4 per cent, managers and officials falling from 7.4 per cent to 6.0 per cent, and craftsmen and foremen falling from 11.2 per cent to 10.3 per cent. The occupations that increased in percentage terms were service, laborers, and operatives occupations. The farmers and farm laborers occupations decreased, reflecting the different demands for labor in the United States, rather than an actual decrease in the number of people who would have been in these occupations if emigration had not occurred.

Changes in the Skill Composition of the
Puerto Rican Labor Force

In order to avoid the problem of transfers of occupations, a consolidation of classifications into skilled and unskilled categories provides a clearer picture of the effect of emigration on the skill level of the labor force. Table 4.7 contains the calculations of the skill-level ratio of the labor force for Puerto Rico for the years 1940, 1950, 1960, and for the Puerto Ricans in the United States for the years 1950 and 1960. The ratios of the combined Puerto Rican population in the United States and on the island are also presented in the table. The combined ratio compared to the actual ratio gives an indication of the effect of emigration on the skill level of the current Puerto Rican labor force. First, the table reveals the general upgrading of the labor force in Puerto Rico during the 1940–1960 period. The ratio of unskilled to skilled workers declined significantly: from 4.96 in 1940 to 3.34 in 1950, and even further, to 2.14, in 1960. The unskilled category includes farm laborers, laborers, operatives, and service workers; the skilled group includes professional and technical craftsmen and foremen, and managerial and official workers.

A comparison of the actual unskilled to skilled worker ratios in the migrant population with the Puerto Rican labor force indicates that the former had a significantly higher ratio than the latter. Table 4.7 shows an expected ratio of 3.52 (if emigration had not occurred) in Puerto Rico in 1950, the ratio for migrants in the United States, which was 4.87, and for migrants and their children in the United States, which was 4.62. The findings is clear: the mi-

TABLE 4.7

SKILL COMPOSITION OF THE MIGRANT AND PUERTO RICAN LABOR FORCE

Different Groups for Selected Years	Unskilled Workers*	Skilled Workers*	Ratio: Column 1/2
Puerto Rican Labor Force			
1940	336,567	67,791	4.96
1950	358,992	107,545	3.34
1960	323,200	150,664	2.14
Puerto Rican Migrants and their Children Born in the United States, Labor Force			
1950	75,730	16,380	4.62
1960	194,904	38,166	5.10
Migrant Labor Force			
1950	70,890	14,545	4.87
1960	184,297	32,480	5.67
Expected Puerto Rican Labor Force			
1950	429,882	122,090	3.52
1960	507,497	183,144	2.77
Migration Stream Labor Force 1957–1961	90,400	23,200	3.90
Migration Stream Net Residents Labor Force	167,500	33,200	5.04
Migration Stream Net Nonresidents Labor Force	76,400	28,500	2.68

* The classification of unskilled laborers included laborers, domestic workers, farm laborers, operatives, and service workers. The skilled labor classification included professional, technical, managerial craftsmen, and foremen. The data are from Table 4.5 and the ramp survey cited in the text.

grant population had a higher unskilled segment of the work force than the expected ratio for Puerto Rico without emigration. Even greater differentials were found for the expected ratio and the migrant ratio in 1960, which were 2.77 and 5.67, respectively. The widening differential reflects the improvement of the skill level of the labor force that occurred during the 1950–1960 period; the ratio decreased from 3.52 to 2.77. But even more it reflects the increasing proportion of unskilled to skilled workers in the migration stream in the 1950–1960 period compared to previous migrations. The trend is even more unusual; statistically, the larger the proportion of skilled personnel in a given population, the greater the probability that a migrant would be skilled. Contrary to this expectation, the exact opposite occurred with the proportion of unskilled increasing throughout the period, causing the differentials in ratios to widen considerably from 1.3 to 2.9 or an increase of over 122 per cent in a decade.

In order to observe the direct impact of emigration on the skill level of the Puerto Rican labor force, a comparison of the expected skill ratio without emigration with the actual ratio existing in Puerto Rico is necessary. Table 4.7 reveals the effect clearly: the ratio declined because of emigration from 3.52 per cent in 1950 to the actual rate of 3.34 per cent, or only 5 per cent. This absence of a significant change does not indicate that the skill ratio of the two groups was not significantly different but that the migrant population was not sufficiently large to affect the ratio significantly. Nevertheless, it still caused an upgrading of the skill ratio of the labor force. The major change in the skill mix occurred in the 1950's because of the large size of the emigration and the significantly different skill ratios among the two sets of populations. The expected ratio was 2.77 and it fell to a low 2.14, reflecting approximately a 23 per cent increase in the skill ratio of the Puerto Rican labor force. This increase is especially striking when compared to the rise in the skill ratio resulting from the investment of the society in human capital (education and other factors), which was only 21 per cent — from 3.52 to 2.77. Thus emigration contributed an equal share to the improvement of the Puerto Rican labor force.

Additional evidence confirming the finding that the migration stream contained a more unskilled proportion of workers than the island of Puerto Rico is available from the ramp survey of people leaving and arriving in Puerto Rico by air for the years 1957 to 1963.

Reverse Migration of Skilled Labor

A comparison of the unskilled to skilled ratio in the six-year ramp survey with the 1960 ratio in Puerto Rico supports the finding (see Table 4.7). The skill ratio of net migrants in 1960 could not be calculated because there was a return flow of skilled labor rather than an outflow. Specifically, 2,300 professional and technical workers and 4,200 managerial workers returned in 1960 and 1,800 professional and 4,600 managerial workers in 1961. The craftsmen classification experienced its smallest outflow, 1,100, in 1961. At the same time there was a net outflow of 19,400 unskilled occupational workers.

Undoubtedly, this return flow of skilled labor and the outflow of unskilled labor contributed significantly to the recent improvement in the skill ratio of the Puerto Rican labor force. The return flow phenomenon of the last few years, since 1957, has consisted of migrants returning to Puerto Rico with some increase in the number of United States workers immigrating to the island. Table 4.7 contains the skill ratio of the five years 1957–1961, breaking down the skill ratio for nonresidents, defined as those persons residing outside of Puerto Rico for one year or more, and the residents. The net movement of nonresidents has been one of immigration back to Puerto Rico, and the net movement of residents has been emigration to the United States. The latter exceeded the former, but in decreasing size each year. The unskilled to skilled ratio of the net nonresidents for the five years of the ramp survey was 2.68 compared to 5.04 for the departing residents. The total combined ratio of both groups was 3.90 compared to 2.14 in Puerto Rico in 1960. Thus, the immigrants had a higher skill composition than the emigrants, and the result of the two-way movement was an upgrading of the labor force in Puerto Rico.

Another criterion of skill level of a population or labor force is the amount of education possessed by the population. The data from the census years, the ramp survey, and Mills' study[11] indicate that the migrants possessed more education (measured in terms of median grades of school completed) than the population on the island. Why has the higher educational attainment not been reflected in a greater number of skilled workers in the migration stream, compared to the number of unskilled workers? Two factors explain the perplexing and seemingly inconsistent problem. One, the educational level of the migrants is not significantly higher than the remaining population in terms of qualifying for more advanced occupations. For example, if the migrants had a seventh-grade education and the Puerto Ricans on the island had a fifth-grade education, neither would be qualified for a craft occupation or anything more complex. Another reason is that the migrants may have a

---

[11] C. Wright Mills, Clarence Senior, Rose Kohn Goldsen, *The Puerto Rican Journey* (New York: Harper and Brothers, 1950), p. 28. The educational level of the migrants in the study was 6.5 grades completed, compared to a lower rate of 3.4 grades for the Puerto Rican population.

higher education than the people in Puerto Rico but a lower education than the people in the United States.[12] The result of both of these factors forces the migrants into unskilled occupations in greater proportion than the skilled occupations. Unless the educational level reaches the minimum qualifying level of the advanced occupations, the migrants will not be able to achieve entrance into these occupations.[13]

It is misleading to compare the educational attainment of the migrants with the total population in Puerto Rico. The migrants, being younger than the large segment of the Puerto Rican population, have had educational opportunities that their parents and grandparents lacked. In short, the educational level of the migrants should be standardized against the educational level of people in Puerto Rico of the same age. This standardization by age would give a real indication of whether the migrants were more educated than their counterparts on the island. The results are quite informative: the median years of education completed by Puerto Ricans

TABLE 4.8

AGE-SPECIFIC EDUCATIONAL ATTAINMENT OF THE MIGRANT AND THE
PUERTO RICAN POPULATION FOR CENSUS YEARS 1950 AND 1960
(*Median grade of school completed*)

Age	Migrants 1960		Puerto Rico 1960		Migrants 1950		Puerto Rico 1950	
	Male	Female	Male	Female	Male	Female	Male	Female
14+	8.2	8.0	6.1	5.6	8.0	7.5	4.6	4.2
14–24	9.0	8.9	7.5	7.7	8.5	8.4	5.9	5.7
25–34	8.3	8.2	8.9	7.0	8.2	7.9	6.0	4.8
35–44	8.0	7.2	5.5	4.8	7.8	7.5	4.6	3.9
45–64	6.9	5.9	4.7	4.5	6.7	5.0	4.3	3.4

Sources: United States Department of Commerce, Bureau of the Census, *Census of Population: 1590 and 1960, General and Detailed Characteristics*, PC(1)53D, PC(1)53B, and *Census of the Population: 1950 and 1960, Puerto Ricans in the United States*, Special Final Report, PC(2)-1D (Washington, D. C.: United States Government Printing Office, 1951, 1953, 1961, 1963).

[12] The educational grade level of migrants in the United States was a median of 8.4 years for males and 8.2 for females, compared to a rate of 10.6 for the United States average.
[13] The availability of an abundance of more educated laborers oftentimes stimulates employers to increase the educational requirements for certain jobs and occupations, thus placing the Puerto Rican migrant with less education at a disadvantage in the loose job market.

residing in the United States in 1960 was 8.2 for males and 8.0 for females. Table 4.8 contains the educational levels of the two groups by age.

Several interesting findings emerge from the comparisons of the educational levels of the two groups standardized by age: (1) the differences between the two groups' level of education is reduced significantly (compare the bottom line of all people 14 or older, unstandardized, with any of the differences in education among the two groups with similar ages); (2) the early group of migrants before 1950 had considerably higher educational levels than the island population (for example, male migrants 14–24 had 8.5 grades, while their counterparts on the island had 5.9 grades); (3) the recent migrants had only slightly higher educations than the remaining population in 1960 (for example, for the male migrants 14–19 the education was 8.8, compared to 7.5 for their counterparts); (4) the educational attainment of the migrants did not increase over time and decreased relative to the educational level of Puerto Rico. The differences between the educational levels would be reduced if we compared the expected level without emigration with the level of the migrants. The latter finding is consistent with the observance of unskilled rural farm laborers dominating the migration stream during the 1950's.

Summary

In summary, the emigration of Puerto Ricans to the United States conformed to the a priori expectations — namely, the size of the labor force decreased significantly and the quality of the labor force increased considerably during the twenty-year period of emigration. If the recent trend of skilled migrants returning increases, the effect of migration will be even more significant on the skill level of the labor force.

The comparison of the migrant population with the Puerto Rican population indicated that (1) the migrants had a larger proportion of labor force members than the population on the island; (2) the migrant population had a greater proportion of unskilled to skilled workers than the ratio that existed on the island and it resulted in a substantial improvement in the quality of the labor force. The dependency proportion of the population in Puerto Rico increased, but not as much as the decrease in the labor force participation rate. The emigration prevented extremely high rates of unemployment from emerging on the island; and if emigration ceases in the 1960's without a concomitant increase in the generation of employment, serious unemployment problems will plague the Puerto Rican economy. Contrary to expectations, emigration had a favorable impact on the labor force, significantly improving its quality and reducing unemployment, but lowering the average educational level slightly.

5

Occupational Labor Mobility

Introduction

According to traditional economic theory, differential wage rates for the same type of labor are a sign of disequilibrium in the labor market. The movement of labor into the high wage area would reduce the differential and restore equilibrium. Most theoretical studies of labor mobility treat labor as a homogeneous factor of production, moving between two areas in response to general levels of wages and unemployment. In reality, labor is quite heterogeneous with respect to motivation, education, skill level, occupation, locational preference, and innumerable other factors. Because of these differences, it seems probable that workers of a given occupation or skill level would respond not to general economic conditions in other areas but to specific conditions of employment and earnings for their particular occupation.[1]

The earlier analysis of the composition of the migrant population indicated that there was a greater proportion of unskilled occupations than skilled occupations compared to the Puerto Rican labor force. The migration hypothesis asserted that the composition of the migrant population with respect to occupations and skill levels would be determined, in part, by the differentials, both absolute and relative, of occupational earnings in the two areas.

The major objective of this chapter is to examine the relationship between the occupational distribution of the migrants and the ab-

[1] For example, a truck driver does not move from New York to California because there are better wages and lower rates of unemployment for tailors, or doctors, and so on.

solute and relative differentials in occupational earnings between the United States and Puerto Rico. There are three major questions to be answered: (1) Did the occupational characteristics of the migrants change during the twenty-year period of emigration? (2) Was the occupational distribution of the migrants related to occupational unemployment and/or earnings differentials? (3) Did the emigration contribute to the reduction of the earnings differentials between the United States and Puerto Rico?

The basic methodology employed to examine the relationship of occupational mobility and occupational earnings differentials is a comparison of the size of the differentials in absolute and relative earnings with the size of the occupational movement at different periods of time. It is not expected that changes in occupational earnings alone would explain yearly changes in the occupational distribution of a given migrant population.[2] If the objective was to observe whether changes in the differentials of occupational earnings and unemployment explained these changes of the occupations in a migrant population, one method would be to propose a functional relationship in a regression model and observe whether the independent variables succeeded in explaining the changes in the dependent variable. Unfortunately, data on the annual occupational distribution of the migrants are not available for the entire period of emigration. The data on the occupational characteristics of the migrants for 1957–1961 do not reflect significant changes in the occupational distribution and do not cover a long enough time period to use regression analysis. Moreover, we are not primarily concerned with annual changes but with the basic determinant of the skill mix of a migrant population. For this purpose, it is sufficient to analyze cross-section data for different periods of time in order to observe if any relationships exist between skill mix and differentials in earnings and unemployment.

[2] Belton Fleisher, "Some Economic Aspects of Puerto Rican Migration," *Review of Economics and Statistics*, Vol. XLV (August 1963), p. 245; also a more complete analysis of the aspects of Puerto Rican migration is given in his unpublished Ph.D. thesis, Stanford University, 1961. Fleisher attempts to explain the net migration of Puerto Ricans to the United States by analyzing the changes in the differentials in earnings and unemployment between the two areas. In addition, he introduces two variables, transportation costs and the number of migrants already in the United States. The major finding is that unemployment differentials succeed in explaining around 70 per cent of the variance in annual fluctuations in net Puerto Rican migration between the years 1945 and 1958.

Occupational Characteristics of the Migrants

Was the skill mix, reflected in the occupational distribution of the migrant population, stable throughout the twenty-year period of emigration? On a priori grounds, one would expect that the skill composition of the earliest migrants would be higher than the later migrants. The theoretical discussion in Chapter 2 pointed out the necessity of possessing a minimum income per capita before emigration would occur. At this level of income, knowledge of alternatives and the costs and benefits of these alternatives would be available to the decision maker. With an unequal income distribution prevailing, the skilled segment of the population would reach this threshold level earlier than the unskilled. If the differentials in absolute and/or relative earnings between the two areas were sufficient to offset the short-run costs of migrating, the skilled would have the first opportunity to move and thus would constitute a larger proportion of the migrant population. The costs of migration and the knowledge of alternatives and their benefits are themselves functions of the number of people who have migrated. Therefore, the first group of migrants, with substantially higher costs of migration in terms of risks and uncertainty, would necessarily have to possess more skills and higher earnings before emigrating. It is expected that, as the costs are reduced and the income of the unskilled approaches the threshold level, the composition of the migrant population will shift to a heavier proportion of unskilled to skilled workers, providing the differentials in absolute and relative earnings are higher for the unskilled occupations than for the skilled.

Does the information available on the characteristics of the Puerto Rican migrants conform to the foregoing a priori expectations? Data on the occupational characteristics of the Puerto Rican migrants prior to 1947 are available from a sample survey of the Puerto Rican population in New York City.[3] The survey was geographically restricted to the two major core areas of Puerto Rican migrant settlements in the city, Spanish Harlem in Manhattan and the Morrisania district in the Bronx. The location of the sample causes a bias with regard to the characteristics of the total Puerto

---

[3] C. Wright Mills, Clarence Senior, and Rose Kohn Goldsen, *The Puerto Rican Journey* (New York: Harper and Brothers, 1950), pp. 22–79. The book contains an abundant amount of valuable social and economic characteristics of the migrants.

Rican population in the United States, although a majority of the migrants (82.9 per cent) lived in New York City at the time of the sample. The bias is reflected in the characteristics of the migrants who resided in the two core areas. The sample survey of migrants in these locations was more likely to overstate the proportion of Puerto Rican Negroes and understate the skill level of the migrants. Skilled personnel are more likely to have the opportunity to leave the depressed slum areas. Despite the bias, explicitly recognized by the authors, the sample survey provides valuable information on the social and economic characteristics of the Puerto Rican migrants.

For analytical purposes, different periods of emigration were arbitrarily classified. The migration prior to 1945 was small and can be typed as an individualized migration in contrast to the large-scale postwar exodus, which can be typed as a group migration. The sample survey conducted in 1947 (hereafter termed Mills' study) will be used as the basis of data on the pre-1945 migration. The justification for using this study for the characteristics of the early migration is that 74 per cent of the sample were migrants who arrived before 1945. A comparison of these migrants and those who left between 1945 and 1950 can be undertaken with the 1950 census report on Puerto Ricans residing in the United States. A noticeable difference between the two groups of migrants is observable, although it is understated because of the overlap of migrants.

Another difficulty emerges when a comparison of the skill mix between the pre- and post-1945 migrants is attempted. Unfortunately, Mills' study does not break down the migrants' occupations by the standard used by the census but instead consolidates the occupations into broad classifications of unskilled, skilled, and semiskilled workers, without any accompanying definitions of the occupations placed in each of the categories. Nevertheless, although a direct quantitative comparison is subject to error, the data provide a basis for conclusions of the changes in skill mix on a qualitative basis. Fortunately, the census data on the occupational characteristics of the 1950 and 1960 migrants are comparable and can be examined for direct quantitative changes in specific occupational groups.

Mills' study discovered that the early migration stream contained a higher proportion of skilled and semiskilled workers and negligible amounts of farm workers and agricultural laborers. The early migrants had a stable employment history and a slightly higher income than the Puerto Rican average. Specifically, their findings were that the sample population contained 19 per cent skilled workers and 21 per cent unskilled workers.[4] Thus they correctly concluded that the migrant population was more skilled than the Puerto Rican population, where the unskilled to skilled ratio in 1940 was 4.96 (one skilled worker to almost five unskilled workers). The difference in the unskilled to skilled ratio between the migrants and the island population is sufficiently large to minimize the possibility that the errors from consolidating the occupations caused the differences.

An examination of the Puerto Rican migrant population residing in the United States based on the 1950 United States census would include five years of the rapid postwar migration and 182,000 out of the 226,000 Puerto Ricans migrating to the United States between 1945 and 1950. Thus, on the basis of the occupational statistics in the 1950 census, we can contrast the large group-migration exodus after 1945 to the small migration stream prior to 1945, with a slight bias toward the characteristics of the pre-1945 migration. A comparison of the census and the Mills study reveals a definite change in the skill mix with the influx of the large numbers of the postwar emigration. The unskilled to skilled ratio of workers in the migrant population in the United States in 1950 was 4.62, significantly higher than the approximate 1.00 ratio found in Mills' sample. Apparently the early postwar migration of 1945–1950 consisted of significantly larger numbers of unskilled than skilled workers. The unskilled to skilled ratio was even higher than the expected ratio of 3.52 had there been no emigration. Thus, while the pre-1945 migrants were more skilled and had higher incomes than the population from which they emerged, the postwar migrants were considerably different, having a greater proportion of unskilled to skilled workers than the remaining population on the island of Puerto Rico.

The change from skilled to unskilled dominance of the migration stream is consistent with the hypothesis that a minimum income is necessary in relation to the costs of migration before people will be able to move. In the case of Puerto Rico, the income per capita prior to 1940 was approximately $125 and for unskilled workers it was below this amount. At the same time, transportation to the United States was expensive and inadequate, and the communications of the skilled migrants in the United States would probably not have been transmitted to the bulk of the unskilled rural

---

[4] *Ibid.*, pp. 35–36. In addition, the sample found 24 per cent white-collar workers, which included professional, technical, and managerial occupations.

population. With the end of World War II, there was improved transportation between the island and the mainland, transport costs were lowered, and more general and better communications prevailed between the migrants and the people on the island. These factors and the rising incomes in Puerto Rico during the war (income per capita increased from $154 to $284 between 1940 and 1947[5]) provided the opportunity for large numbers of unskilled and rural segments of the population to respond to the economic opportunities in the United States.

The changes in the occupational composition of the migrant population during the decade of the 1950's can be examined using the two United States census reports of Puerto Ricans born in Puerto Rico and residing in the United States. The major limitation of this comparison is the possibility that the migrants in 1950 upgraded their skills and changed occupations during their ten years of working in the United States. This would tend to overstate the skill level of the migrants who emigrated between 1950 and 1960. On the other hand, interviews with directors of the migration division in New York City indicate that there has been little occupational upgrading among the migrants.[6] Supplementary data on the occupational structure of the migrants during the late 1950's are available from the ramp survey conducted under the auspices of the Puerto Rican government. Economic and social characteristics of the people who arrived and departed from Puerto Rico by air[7] have been collected from a sample survey for the past six years, 1957–1963. This type of data avoids the two basic problems of potential upgrading and shifting of occupations, although not skill levels, when migrating to a more industrialized economy.

[5] Commonwealth of Puerto Rico, Office of the Governor, Puerto Rico Planning Board, Bureau of Economic Statistics, 1962, *Selected Indices of Social and Economic Progress, Fiscal Years 1939–40, 1946–62* (San Juan, Commonwealth of Puerto Rico, 1962).

[6] The director of employment in the department of migration in New York City indicated that from his experience very few Puerto Rican migrants have the opportunity or the desire to learn new skills and upgrade their economic positions. The migrants try to emphasize to their children the value of working hard in school to advance themselves economically. The migrants are content to hold down decent jobs and support their families. Most do not have the time to worry about job advancement but hope that economic success will come to their children.

[7] Commonwealth of Puerto Rico, Department of Labor, Bureau of Labor Statistics, 1957–1962, *Characteristics of Passengers Who Traveled by Air Between Puerto Rico and the United States* (San Juan, Commonwealth of Puerto Rico, 1957–1962).

The comparison of the unskilled to skilled ratio of migrants in the United States in 1960 with those in 1950 show a continuation of the dominance of the unskilled workers in the migration stream. In 1960 the ratio of unskilled to skilled workers was 5.67, compared to a ratio of 4.87 in 1950. This represents an increase of 16 per cent within a decade, and there is a possibility of underestimating this change if occupational upgrading of the 1950 migrants had occurred. In either event, the evidence indicates that the most recent migrants had a higher proportion of unskilled to skilled workers than the earlier migrants prior to 1950. These results are even more striking in light of labor market studies that indicate that skilled workers are considered more mobile than unskilled and the labor force in Puerto Rico has become more skilled during the past twenty years. The expected skill ratio in Puerto Rico, with the assumption of the absence of emigration, was 2.77, considerably below the 5.67 ratio of the migrant population. Thus the composition of the migrant population has become more unskilled, especially in contrast to the upgraded skill level of the Puerto Rican population.

The ramp survey data on the unskilled to skilled ratio confirms the census findings: the ratio of residents departing for the United States for the years 1957–1961 was 5.04. Table 5.1 contains specific ratios of the number of farm laborers to professional personnel and

TABLE 5.1

SKILL RATIO: UNSKILLED TO SKILLED WORKERS IN THE MIGRATION STREAM AND PUERTO RICO FOR THE 1957–1961 PERIOD

Year	Puerto Rico (Farm Laborers/Professional)	Migrants	Puerto Rico (Farm Laborers/Craftsmen)	Migrants
1957	3.77	9.71	2.22	5.23
1958	3.39	2.46	2.11	5.96
1959	2.96	6.00	1.95	4.60
1960	2.61	7.20*	1.80	15.18
1961	2.58	9.50*	1.70	4.30

* There was a return flow of professional workers in these two years, which means that for every one professional that returned to Puerto Rico there were 7.2 farm laborers who left the island in 1960 and 9.5 in 1961. The above ratios were calculated for the net migration of both residents and nonresidents.

Source: Commonwealth of Puerto Rico, Department of Labor, Bureau of Labor Statistics, Characteristics of the Passengers Who Travel by Air Between Puerto Rico and the United States (San Juan, Commonwealth of Puerto Rico, 1957–1962).

to craftsmen in the migration stream compared to the same ratios existing in Puerto Rico. Although the ratios fluctuate considerably, the differences are quite pronounced for every year. Specifically, the ratio of farm laborers to professional and technical, with the exception of 1958, ranged between 6.00 to 9.71, compared to the ratio on the island of 3.77 to 2.58. Incidentally, the ratios calculated for the island were only the employed labor force in contrast to the migrant population which was total labor force. The same pattern exists between the farm laborers and craftsmen, except that the ratio differences are smaller. It is important to note that the last two years of the table, 1960 and 1961, show a return flow of professional and technical workers. This emphasizes the preponderance of the unskilled in the recent emigration.

Table 5.2 presents the occupational distribution of those who migrated to the United States between 1957 and 1961, based on the total population who migrated. In 1960, the percentage of their occupations considered to be skilled was 7.8 per cent, compared to a percentage of 29.7 considered to be unskilled,[8] or approximately four unskilled to one skilled worker in the migrant stream. The ramp survey also reveals a heavy proportion of farm laborers in the migration stream. The average for the five-year period showed that farm laborers comprised 17 per cent of the total migrant population. Operatives were the next most common occupation emigrating, accounting for 9 per cent, followed by clerical and sales occupations with 4.5 per cent of the total migrant population. The skilled groups of craftsmen and foremen and professional and technical workers accounted for only 3.5 per cent and 2.5 per cent, respectively. Negligible amounts of service workers (domestic and protective workers) and farmers and farm managers were in the migration stream during this period of time.

In contrast to the Mills study, the ramp survey data covering the migrants during the past six years indicate that a significant change in the occupational composition of the migrant stream occurred between the prewar and postwar period. The latter period contained a substantially large proportion of farm laborers (35 per cent) of the total labor force migrating during the past five years, in contrast to Mills' finding of negligible numbers of farm laborers prior

[8] Skilled occupations were defined as professional, technical, managerial and official, craftsmen and foremen, while the unskilled occupational classification included operatives, service workers, laborers, and farm laborers.

TABLE 5.2

OCCUPATIONAL DISTRIBUTION OF RESIDENTS* WHO EMIGRATED
FROM PUERTO RICO 1957–1961

(*Percentages*)

Occupation	1957	1958	1959	1960	1961
Professional and Technical	2.7	2.8	3.4	2.6	5.4
Owners, Managers, and Officials	0.2	0.3	0.2	0.9	0.4
Clerical and Sales	1.8	3.2	2.2	0.6	2.6
Craftsmen and Foremen	5.0	2.6	6.5	4.3	5.1
Operatives	8.2	10.1	9.8	7.0	9.2
Domestic Service	0.7	0.7	0.7	0.7	0.7
Protective Service	0.1	0.1	0.4	0.3	0.4
All Other Service	2.3	1.8	3.0	2.5	2.0
Farm Laborers	16.7	18.2	15.0	17.7	13.2
Laborers	1.4	2.5	2.1	1.5	1.8
Others Not in the Labor Force	57.0	52.7	52.8	54.0	54.0

* Residents are defined as persons who resided in Puerto Rico for one year or more.

Source: Commonwealth of Puerto Rico, Department of Labor, Bureau of Labor Statistics, *Characteristics of Passengers Who Travel by Air Between Puerto Rico and the United States* (San Juan, Commonwealth of Puerto Rico, 1957–1962).

to 1945.[9] Thus, not only has the skill level changed considerably but the absence of farm laborers in the prewar migration was offset by the large postwar migration of rural farm laborers. This conforms to the hypothesis: the rural farm workers, usually being the poorest and least informed, would be the last segment of the population to migrate; but because of the economic advantages that migration offers them, they eventually dominate the composition of the migration stream.[10]

[9] It is possible that migrants in Mills' sample may have misinterpreted the question and answered with the occupation they are presently employed at in the United States rather than the occupation they had in Puerto Rico. This would understate the actual number of migrants who were farm laborers; that is, very few farm laborers live in New York City.

[10] The exact timing of the movement of farm laborers to the United States is difficult to establish because data of occupations at the time of departure for the United States are not available before 1957. Nevertheless, some indication of the timing can be uncovered from the data on agricultural employment in Puerto Rico. It began to decrease in absolute numbers in 1949–1950, falling from 216,000 workers in 1949–1959 to 172,000 in 1953, and continued thereafter to fall rapidly. The relatively small generation of employment in the other sectors leads one to conclude that many of the new migrants were from

As it is to be expected, the different geographical origins of the migrants during the two periods also brought about differences in other characteristics of the migrants. With regard to sex character- istics, the pre-1945 migrants had a preponderance of women. In 1940 the sex ratio on the island of Puerto Rico was even, that is, 100 males for every 100 females. The sex ratio in urban centers on the island was 83 men to 100 women; but, in contrast, Mills' study found a sex ratio of Puerto Ricans in New York City of 63 males to 100 females. The change in the composition of the migrant stream has corrected the imbalance, bringing the sex ratio of the migrants in the United States in 1950 to 92.3 males to 100 females,[11] almost approaching the even ratio in Puerto Rico in 1950. The data from the ramp survey covering the five years 1957–1961 reveal that the bulk of the migrants were males, 106,220 out of 116,400, or 91 per cent of the total migrants.

The previous chapter discussed the differences in education among the early and recent migrants. In Mills' study the education of migrants measured by median grades completed was 6.5,[12] com- pared to the 1960 census data of 8.5 grades completed by migrants. Again a significant change in educational attainment of the migrants of different periods emerges.

The only basic similarity between the two migrant groups was the age of the migrants; both groups consisted of young productive members of the population. The majority of the migrants fell be- tween the ages of 15 to 39. This conforms to the expectation that emigration is a youthful phenomenon and allows individuals to maximize the present discounted value of their future income stream by taking advantage of the income differentials between two areas. Mills' study reported that 61 per cent of the migrants were between the ages of 18 to 39,[13] while the ramp survey data indicated that 52 per cent of the number of residents who departed from Puerto Rico were between the ages of 15 to 34.

The heavy predominance of male migration in the ramp survey

---

the labor force in agriculture. The income per capita rose during the same period of time from $328 to $475, thus providing a higher income and enabling more farm workers to emigrate.

[11] United States Department of Commerce, Bureau of the Census, *Census of Population: 1950*, Special Report P-E 3D, *Puerto Ricans in the Continental United States*, p. 3D-5 (Washington, D. C.: United States Government Printing Office, 1953).

[12] Mills, Senior, and Goldsen, *op. cit.*, p. 30.

[13] *Ibid.*, p. 28.

points directly to the fact that very few women are engaged in farm occupations. In summary, it appears that the migration stream of the late 1950's consisted primarily of young male agricultural workers, in contrast to the pre-1947 migration of female urban semi-skilled industrial workers.

Differentials in Occupational Earnings

Was the composition of the occupational structure of the migrant population related to the size of the differentials of occupational earnings between the United States and Puerto Rico? Fortunately, data are available on occupational earnings in New York City, the location where the majority of migrants reside, and occupational earnings in Puerto Rico for the period 1952–1962. The most useful statistics on earnings, for our purposes, would have been occupational earnings for Puerto Ricans in the United States. The New York City data are the closest approximation to the earnings of Puerto Ricans in the United States. Although the data used probably overstate the differentials of earnings of Puerto Ricans in the United States compared to Puerto Rico, they still reflect basic differentials in occupational earnings between the two areas. In addition, if Puerto Ricans respond to the general conditions existing for a given occupation rather than to the specific earnings of Puerto Ricans in the same occupation, the weakness of the data is substantially reduced.

Before proceeding to analyze the data on occupational earnings, it is necessary to point out the differences in the occupational categories of the United States and Puerto Rico. The craftsmen and foremen workers' classifications are almost comparable, with only a slight bias in underestimating the wages of the craftsmen in the United States (the earnings of the building trades are excluded in the United States data[14]). The United States category (New York City) of custodial and material movement occupations is most directly comparable to unskilled occupational classifications in Puerto Rico. Occupations such as farm laborers, laborers, domestic workers, operatives, and service workers in Puerto Rico are most likely to find employment in the custodial category in the United States.

---

[14] Building trades hourly and weekly earnings are usually higher than craftsmen working in factories. The seasonal nature of the former employment probably brings the two groups' annual earnings closer together.

The entrance of unskilled Puerto Rican migrants into custodial occupations such as porters, janitors, elevator operators, cleaners, laborers, guards, and so on can be filled with a minimum of training. Since it is easy to move from one set of unskilled occupations to another, the earnings of these two groups of occupations were considered relevant for comparative purposes. On this basis, two separate categories of Puerto Rican occupations were compared to the earnings of custodial and movement occupations in the United States: (1) farm laborers and (2) operatives and service workers.

The calculations of the absolute occupational earnings differentials in terms of dollars and percentages between New York City and Puerto Rico are presented in Table 5.3.[15] The migration hypothesis asserted that the members of the occupations with the greatest absolute and relative occupational earnings differentials would migrate in greater numbers than those in other occupations with smaller differentials in earnings. The data in Table 5.3 indicate that the occupation with the greatest differential in percentage terms throughout the 1950's was the farm laborers. Occupational wage data for the period prior to 1950 was not available for both areas. The differential earnings in percentage terms between farm laborers' earnings and custodial occupations are presented in columns E and F in Table 5.3. Negligible amounts of migrants from Puerto Rico enter farm laborers' occupations in the United States. Most farm laborers from Puerto Rico are temporary seasonal farm migrants who return to Puerto Rico after the harvest season for east-coast crops. Therefore, instead of using farm laborers' earnings, custodial occupations earnings were selected because it was the type of permanent job that unskilled farm laborers from Puerto Rico would find in the United States. The percentage differentials in earnings ranged from an extremely high difference of 928 per cent in 1952 to a low of 519 per cent in 1956. Throughout most of the decade the differential averaged close to 600 per cent. This differential was significantly larger than any other occupational differ-

---

[15] The higher cost of living in the New York area compared to Puerto Rico would lower all the occupational earnings differentials. If larger differences in cost of living for the more unskilled occupations exist, this would tend to reduce the earnings differentials for the unskilled more than for the skilled occupations. However, the earnings differentials between the unskilled and skilled were sufficiently large to dismiss the effect of differences in the cost of living from significantly affecting the rank order of the size of occupational earnings differentials.

TABLE 5.3

ABSOLUTE DIFFERENTIALS IN OCCUPATIONAL EARNINGS BETWEEN PUERTO RICO AND NEW YORK CITY 1952–1962
(Median weekly earnings in dollar and percentage terms)

	Professional		Craftsmen		Custodial	Farm	Custodial	Operatives and Service	Office	Clerical and Sales
Year	United States	Puerto Rico	United States	Puerto Rico	United States	Puerto Rico	United States	Puerto Rico	United States	Puerto Rico
	A	B	C	D	E	F	G	H	I	J
1952	$51.04	243%	$51.10	310%	$53.00	928%	$46.30	453%	$30.46	222%
1953	54.85	250	54.40	316	52.40	670	47.60	440	31.25	223
1954	56.52	245	58.10	328	51.80	563	48.85	445	34.23	229
1955	61.80	255	61.30	333	53.70	602	48.65	409	35.89	224
1956	62.75	260	60.50	300	54.90	519	50.15	381	36.88	221
1957	61.85	234	64.50	308	59.30	582	52.00	365	38.77	220
1958	71.75	259	64.90	291	62.30	530	55.50	360	40.35	222
1959	69.85	242	63.30	260	64.10	561	53.60	319	37.50	200
1960	71.25	242	67.30	265	68.90	697	54.50	310	38.22	201
1961	68.20	224	70.40	272	68.10	551	56.80	315	44.43	218
1962	66.20	211	76.60	292	72.60	676	57.45	307	45.82	218

Sources: United States Department of Labor, Bureau of Labor Statistics, *Occupational Wage Survey,* Bulletin Series 1000+ (Washington, D. C.: United States Government Printing Office, 1952–1962). Commonwealth of Puerto Rico, Department of Labor, Bureau of Labor Statistics, *Employment, Hours and Earnings in Puerto Rico* (San Juan, Commonwealth of Puerto Rico, 1952–1962).

ential throughout the period. During the same period of time the percentage of farm laborers who migrated was larger than any other occupational grouping, thus supporting the hypothesis.

The professional earnings differential ranged from a high of 260 per cent in 1956 to a low of 211 per cent in 1962. The lowest differential between the clerical and sales workers' earnings in Puerto Rico and the office workers' earnings in New York City ranged from a high of 229 per cent in 1954 to a low of 200 per cent in 1959. The occupation with the second largest differential in earnings was the relatively unskilled classification of operatives and service workers compared with custodial earnings in New York City. The highest differential was 453 per cent in 1952, and the lowest 307 per cent in 1962. The differential in craftsmen's earnings in the two areas was higher than the professional classification earnings differential, ranging from a high of 333 per cent in 1955 to a low of 291 per cent in 1958.

These findings of the sizes of the differentials among occupational earnings in Puerto Rico and New York City support the hypothesis that the composition of the migration stream will be determined by the sizes of the absolute differentials (in percentage terms) among occupations. The farm laborers had the greatest absolute earnings advantage of emigrating and did so in the greatest number. The relatively unskilled occupations of operatives and service workers had the next largest differential and also were the second largest occupation within the migration stream. Craftsmen had a higher differential in earnings than professional people and migrated in greater numbers than the professional occupations. In conclusion, it appears that if each occupational group possesses knowledge of the alternatives (that is, if it has a given income level), the occupational structure of the migration stream will be determined, in part, by the absolute differentials in occupational earnings in the two areas.

In terms of absolute dollar differentials, the professional and craftsmen occupational groups had the largest differential, but surprisingly enough the differentials between the custodial and farm laborers were only slightly below the other two groups. (See columns A, C, E in Table 5.3 for comparisons.)

The changes in the absolute occupational earnings differentials provide a basis for a qualitative statement that occupational mobility corresponds to specific changes in differentials in occupational earnings. The data indicate that the occupational structure of the migrants contained an increasing proportion of farm laborers and a decreasing proportion of skilled professional workers and operatives. The changes in the occupational earnings differentials conformed to these changes in the structure of the migrant population. The professional earnings differential decreased from 250 per cent in 1953 to 211 per cent in 1962, and the occupation lost numbers in 1957–1959, but had a return flow in 1960–1962. The operatives' differential decreased from 453 per cent in 1952 to 305 per cent in 1962, while their percentage in the migrant population also decreased from 10 per cent in 1957–1958 to 7.5 per cent in 1960–1962. The stability of the differential earnings of clerical and sales workers over the ten-year period is reflected in the stability of the percentage of this occupation in the ramp survey for the period 1957–1961. There was similar stability in both earnings differentials and percentage of the migrant population for the craftsmen and foremen.

Thus the occupational earnings of the workers in New York City and Puerto Rico are related to and contribute to the type of occupational composition of the migrant stream. The changes in these earnings differentials of the occupations seem to have influenced the proportions of the occupations in the migrant population. In short, those occupations that have the greatest absolute differentials in earnings will constitute the largest proportions of the migrant population, if the members of the occupation possess the necessary income to emigrate.

Perhaps a more relevant comparison of occupational wages for Puerto Ricans would be the wages in industries and occupations where Puerto Rican migrants have found employment in the past. Many Puerto Rican migrants have secured employment in the garment industry in New York City. A comparison of the wages in this industry, which is one of the lower paying industries in the country, with occupations in Puerto Rico support the previous data. Sewing machine operators in 1951 in the garment industry in New York City earned $2.14 per hour or $85.60 for a forty-hour week. Male workers in classifications of packers, clerks, and movers in the same industry earned $1.40 per hour or $56.00 per forty-hour week. Hand sewers earned $1.45 per hour or $58.00 per forty-hour week.[16] This

[16] United States Department of Labor, Bureau of Labor Statistics, Special Regional Report, Middle Atlantic Regional Office, New York, 1962, *Employment, Earnings and Wages in New York City, 1950–1960* (Washington, D. C.: U.S. Government Printing Office, 1960).

latter job could easily be performed by domestic needleworkers in Puerto Rico with a minimum of training. Puerto Rican home needle workers earned only $6.05 per week, and farm workers earned $6.40 per week in 1951.

Clearly, the unskilled Puerto Rican workers, if they emigrated, could have earned eight to nine times the absolute incomes earned in Puerto Rico. Additional comparisons with other industries and unskilled occupational earnings in the United States follow the same pattern with even greater differentials. This large absolute differential for unskilled workers was sufficient to cause a large number of these unskilled workers to migrate to New York City in order to capitalize on the large differentials in earnings between the two areas.

The migration hypothesis also asserted that those occupations or skill levels that had the greatest relative earnings differentials would comprise the majority of the occupational distribution of the migrants. In other words, workers respond to relative economic opportunities in addition to absolute economic differentials. Table 5.4, columns A, C, E, contains median weekly earnings of the different occupations in New York City, while columns B, D, F, G contain median weekly earnings of occupations in Puerto Rico. The narrower skill differentials in the United States compared to Puerto Rico are evident from the data in the columns. Since the skill differentials are lower in the United States than in Puerto Rico, it means that unskilled workers can considerably improve their relative economic positions if they emigrate to the United States. For example, in the United States earnings in the professional occupations in 1951 were $78 per week compared to $57.20 for the custodial occupations, while in Puerto Rico the differential between professional ($35.60) earnings and farm laborers' earnings ($6.40) was considerably greater than the United States differential.

Comparing the differentials in the United States between skilled and custodial earnings, we find the professional earnings 1.46 times greater than custodial earnings in 1952, while in Puerto Rico the earnings of professional people were 5.56 times greater than farm laborers and 2.71 times as great as operatives and service earnings.

A comparison of the earnings of craftsmen with custodians in the United States gives a skill differential earnings of 1.27, while in Puerto Rico in 1952 the ratio of earnings of craftsmen to farm laborers was 3.79 and for operatives and service workers, 1.85. The ratios are all presented in Table 5.5. The data clearly show that

TABLE 5.4

WEEKLY EARNINGS BY OCCUPATION FOR PUERTO RICO AND NEW YORK CITY

(*In dollars*)

Year	Professional and Technical		Craftsmen and Foremen		Custodial	Farm Laborers	Operatives and Service
	New York City A	Puerto Rico B	New York City C	Puerto Rico D	New York City E	Puerto Rico F	Puerto Rico G
1951	78.00	n.a.*	71.20	n.a.	57.20	n.a.	n.a.
1952	86.64	35.60	75.40	24.30	59.40	6.40	13.10
1953	91.25	36.40	79.60	25.20	61.60	9.20	14.00
1954	95.62	39.10	83.60	25.50	63.00	11.20	14.15
1955	100.00	39.20	87.60	26.30	64.40	10.70	15.75
1956	101.75	39.00	90.80	30.30	68.00	13.10	17.85
1957	107.75	45.90	94.00	30.50	71.60	12.30	19.60
1958	116.75	45.00	98.80	33.90	76.80	14.50	21.30
1959	118.75	48.90	102.80	39.50	78.00	13.90	24.40
1960	121.25	50.00	108.00	40.70	80.40	11.50	25.90
1961	123.00	54.80	111.20	40.80	83.20	15.10	26.40
1962	125.50	59.30	116.40	39.80	85.20	12.60	27.75

* n.a. = not available
Sources: Same as Table 4.12.

OCCUPATIONAL LABOR MOBILITY

TABLE 5.5

OCCUPATIONAL EARNINGS DIFFERENTIALS WITHIN THE UNITED STATES
AND PUERTO RICO FOR SELECTED YEARS 1952 AND 1962
(*Percentages*)

Year	United States	Puerto Rico	Puerto Rico
	Professional and Technical/ Custodial	*Professional and Technical/Farm Laborers*	*Professional and Technical/Operatives and Service*
1952	1.46	5.56	2.71
1962	1.47	4.70	2.13
	Craftsmen/ Custodial	*Craftsmen/Farm Laborers*	*Craftsmen/Operatives and Service*
1952	1.27	3.79	1.85
1962	1.36	3.16	1.43

Sources: Same as Table 4.11.

the skill earnings differentials in the area of immigration (the United States) were considerably lower than the area of emigration (Puerto Rico), thus giving the unskilled workers a greater incentive on a relative basis for emigrating to the United States during the decade of the 1950's.

The skill differentials decreased significantly in Puerto Rico, as is expected as the economy grows rapidly and reaches an industrialized stage, but the differentials between the United States and Puerto Rico remained sufficiently large to reinforce the movement of unskilled workers in greater proportion than skilled as a response to greater absolute and relative earnings in the United States. It is interesting to note that one of the factors contributing to the decline in the proportion of operatives and service workers in the migration stream (as seen in the ramp survey data) may have been the complete reduction of the relative differentials between operatives and service workers compared to craftsmen in Puerto Rico in 1962. The differential in earnings in Puerto Rico was 1.43 compared to a differential in the United States between craftsmen and custodial workers of 1.36. In contrast, the ratio of earnings of farm workers to professionals and farm workers to craftsmen in Puerto Rico compared to the earnings ratio of custodial workers to professionals and craftsmen in the United States was significantly different in 1962: 4.70 in Puerto Rico to 1.47 in the United States, and 3.16 compared to 1.36, respectively.

In summary, the large absolute and relative differentials for occupational earnings of skill levels between the United States and Puerto Rico were major factors determining the occupational structure of the migrant labor force. The greater differentials both in absolute and relative terms for the unskilled workers stimulated a greater proportional movement of these occupations which clearly dominated the migrant population throughout the period of large-scale, massive emigration, 1945–1960. The combination of decreasing absolute differentials and the favorable relative earnings differential in Puerto Rico may have accounted for the observed return flow of greater numbers of skilled migrants in the last few years. The gross movement of people into and out of Puerto Rico reveals that the return flow is growing larger each year, reducing the net outflow.

But, even more significant is the fact that the return flow contained a greater proportion of skilled than unskilled workers. The net migration figures still indicate an outflow of all occupations with the exception of professional, technical, and managerial manpower in the last three years, which was sufficiently large to offset the outflow in these occupations. It seems that the existence of absolute differentials for skilled labor was not the only factor needed to attract and/or keep the skilled personnel in the past three years. Apparently the relative economic position in Puerto Rico, with its concomitant social and community status, compensated for the decreases in absolute earnings upon returning to Puerto Rico. It is also possible that the rate of compensation and promotion of workers with scarce skills is better in a rapidly growing economy and may account for the return migration, in anticipation of longer-run economic benefits. In any event, the existence of absolute, positive differentials between the United States and Puerto Rico would not account for the return flow of migrants to Puerto Rico,[17] but the inclusion of relative differentials as a factor in mobility helps to explain this unusual reverse movement.

The multiple factors stimulating a worker and/or his family to move into a new, strange, and often hostile environment are complex and difficult to isolate and understand. Many other non-economic factors contribute to the decision whether to migrate or

[17] It is possible for the absolute income differentials proposition to be valid if a certain threshold level of absolute differentials is required to stimulate emigration. If the absolute differential dropped below this level, emigration would cease. In the case of Puerto Rico the differentials did not seem to decrease significantly to justify a reversal of the skilled labor back to Puerto Rico.

not. The previous analysis does not mean to imply that economic factors were the only motives for migration. But apparently in the case of the postwar Puerto Rican emigration, it appears that the large absolute and relative earnings differentials between occupations accounts for the type of occupational distribution in the migration stream.

Occupational Unemployment Differentials

Do workers respond to unemployment differentials between two areas? Specifically, do workers migrate to areas where the unemployment rates of other migrants are lower than the unemployment rates in their home country and/or do workers of a given occupation respond to differential occupational unemployment rates? Belton Fleisher, in an analysis of annual and quarterly fluctuations of Puerto Rican migration to the United States for the 1946–1958 period, discovered that unemployment differentials, specifically the rate of unemployment in the United States, were the major factor explaining the fluctuations in migration. The inclusion of wage differentials did not contribute to an explanation of the annual and quarterly fluctuations in Puerto Rican migration to the United States.[18] The study used the rates of unemployment in the United States as a whole, compared to Puerto Rico.

An examination of the rates of unemployment of Puerto Ricans in the United States for the census years 1950 and 1960 compared with the unemployment rates in Puerto Rico reveals that in 1950, during a year of rapid emigration, the United States unemployment rate for Puerto Ricans was 15 per cent compared to 13 per cent in Puerto Rico and in 1960 the unemployment rate for Puerto Ricans in the United States remained quite high — 10 per cent compared to a rate of 13 per cent on the island. Apparently the high rate of unemployment for fellow Puerto Ricans was either

[18] Belton Fleisher, *op. cit.*, p. 245. While Fleisher's analysis explains the net movement of Puerto Ricans to the United States for the period 1945–1958 by the fluctuations in unemployment differentials, it is not clear that the additional years 1958–1963 would conform to the findings for the previous years. The large return flow phenomenon may not be easily explained merely with the use of unemployment differentials. In addition, the movement of residents (Puerto Ricans residing in Puerto Rico for a year or more) who migrated during the 1957–1963 period does not seem to be decreasing in number, despite high unemployment rates during this period in the United States. The resident net migrants do not seem to be responding to job vacancies in the United States, as the net migrant figures indicate prior to 1957.

not known to the migrants or was not considered an important factor in deciding to emigrate. It would appear that the migrants did not respond to job vacancies for Puerto Ricans; instead they either responded to the general level of unemployment in New York or in the United States or decided that the benefits of migration from extremely high earnings differentials were sufficient to offset the costs. The higher the unemployment rate for Puerto Ricans in the United States, the greater the cost of migration. Apparently the optimistic and ambitious character of people undertaking a significant change in their lives, such as migrating to a foreign area, enables them to minimize the expected possibility of unemployment and maximize the expected gain in income by securing a job in a relatively short period of time.

It is interesting to note that the use of relevant unemployment rates, those rates that directly affect the migrants, did not give the same result as the unemployment rate for the United States for all workers. Labor market studies[19] have found that one of the most common and effective methods of obtaining job information and securing employment is through direct communication with friends and relatives. The extent and reliability of the information is usually superior to alternative methods of communication. This type of communication should prevail with greater use and strength when large international-type migratory movements are involved. With the knowledge of the difficulties of securing employment available from reliable sources, it is even more surprising that emigration continued throughout the decade. Apparently the subjective risk of not finding employment is substantially outweighed by the economic advantages existing in the United States. The narrowing of the absolute and relative earning differentials apparently has reduced the size of the migration stream considerably, especially during the last few years. The rate during the fifties averaged close to 50,000 migrants per year, while it dropped to 10,000 migrants in the first three years of the 1960's.

The migrants did not respond to the general rate of unemployment for all Puerto Ricans in the United States, nor did they respond to unemployment rates by occupations as they did to earnings differentials by occupation. Data on unemployment rates for Puerto Ricans in the United States by occupation are not available. Instead, a comparison of unemployment rates by occupation for the United

[19] Charles A. Myers and George P. Shultz, *The Dynamics of a Labor Market* (New York: Prentice Hall, Inc., 1951), pp. 47–49.

States and for Puerto Rico will be examined. The unemployment rates by occupation for the United States for Puerto Ricans should be expected to be higher than the general United States rates because of (1) the last hired, first laid off policy; (2) possible discrimination, and (3) lower skill levels of Puerto Ricans in each occupation. In any event, Table 5.6 reveals that in 1950 every

TABLE 5.6

OCCUPATIONAL UNEMPLOYMENT RATES IN PUERTO RICO AND THE
UNITED STATES FOR SELECTED YEARS 1950 AND 1960
(Percentages)

	1960		1950	
Occupation	Puerto Rico	United States	Puerto Rico	United States
Professional and Technical	1.4	1.5	1.6	2.2
Farmers and Farm Managers	0.8	0.3	0.5	0.3
Owners, Managers, and Officials	1.5	1.2	1.2	1.7
Clerical and Kindred	3.4	3.6	2.9	3.5
Sales	4.3	3.4	4.0	4.0
Craftsmen and Foremen	7.7	5.4	9.0	6.9
Operatives	8.2	8.0	4.2	7.8
Domestic Service	4.2	3.7	2.8	4.7
All Other Service	5.6	5.6	3.7	7.1
Farm Laborers	2.4	5.4	2.2	5.4
Laborers	10.0	11.4	10.0	14.3

Unemployment rates are for the experienced civilian labor force for each occupational classification.

Sources: United States Department of Commerce, Bureau of the Census, Census of Population: 1950 and 1960, Puerto Rico and Census of Population: 1950 and 1960, Puerto Ricans in the United States (Washington, D. C.: United States Government Printing Office, 1951, 1953, 1961, 1963).

occupation in the United States (with the exception of craftsmen) had a higher unemployment rate than the comparable occupations in Puerto Rico. Part of this phenomenon may result from the fact that emigration from 1945–1950 may have reduced some of the measured unemployment in Puerto Rico. Nevertheless, the job vacancy hypothesis is subject to some serious questioning.[20] The

20 Mills' study reported that only 4 per cent of the migrants in the labor force were unemployed in Puerto Rico: 2 per cent were males unemployed in the labor force in Puerto Rico and 6 per cent were females. A total of 71

Puerto Rican migrants seem to be moving not in response to greater employment opportunities — in fact, they are moving into worse employment opportunities — but in response to significantly greater absolute and relative earnings differentials from prospective jobs. The latter differentials are sufficient to compensate for the higher costs of migration due to higher rates of unemployment for occupations and for Puerto Ricans.

Summary

In summary, the absolute and relative occupational earnings differentials between United States and Puerto Rico contributed to the determination of the occupational distribution of the migrant population. The greatest differentials existed for the unskilled workers who responded by comprising the heaviest proportion of the migrant labor force during the period of large-scale emigration, 1945–1960. The differentials were sufficient to compensate for the increased costs of migration due to higher unemployment rates for Puerto Ricans in general and for specific occupations. The composition of the migrant stream over time became increasingly dominated by unskilled workers. The findings support the migration hypothesis with regard to the minimum income concept necessary before emigration occurs, with the differentials, both absolute and relative, determining emigration and the occupational composition of the migrant population.

---

per cent of the sample had a full uninterrupted year of employment in an economy marked by sharp seasonal unemployment. Apparently, migration was not in response to better employment only.

6

An Analysis of the Effects of the Quality of Labor on the Growth of Output and Productivity

Introduction

Prior to the large-scale emigration of Puerto Ricans to the United States in 1946, the Puerto Rican economy underwent significant changes between 1940 and 1945. In 1940 the Popular Democratic Party came into power and, with the guidance and aid of the United States representative to Puerto Rico, Rexford Tugwell, it instituted a series of major social, political, and economic reforms.[1] Muñoz-Marín, the present governor of Puerto Rico, and a group of energetic Puerto Rican leaders, aided by a staff of United States advisors, especially economists, initiated and directed the program "Operation Bootstrap." The program was designed to raise the standard of living of the population of Puerto Rico and erase the stigma of the "poorhouse of the Caribbean" associated with the island.

The involvement of the United States in World War II stimulated a large-scale investment program in Puerto Rico in the form of military bases and production of goods for the war effort. The investment served as a major factor in stimulating the stagnating

[1] Harvey Perloff, *Puerto Rico's Economic Future* (Chicago, Ill.: University of Chicago Press, 1959). The book contains a detailed account of the economic changes and reforms that occurred during the 1940–1947 period. Two major governmental activities during this period were the land reform and the establishment of a government industrial development company, "Fomento."

agricultural economy on the path of successful economic development. The combination of the self-help effort on the part of the Puerto Rican people and leaders and the significant United States investment in Puerto Rico during the war years provided the "big push" needed to stimulate the growth of the poverty-ridden economy. The large-scale development of social overhead capital and the construction of modern factories during the war laid the foundation for the future growth of the economy.

At the same time that encouraging signs of successful economic growth were observed in Puerto Rico, a dangerous threat emerged in the form of rapid population growth on the island during the 1940–1947 period. The large-scale emigration, which commenced in 1946, fortunately served as a positive check on the population growth, preventing high unemployment and allowing gains in output to be translated into per capita income increases. While emigration eliminated the dangers of rapid population growth, it did not have a significantly negative effect on the growth of output because of the redundancy of the large proportion of the emigrants. On the contrary, the movement of predominantly unskilled emigrants raised the skill composition of the labor force, which may have contributed to increased output per worker on the island.

The principal objective of this chapter is to explore the rapid growth of output throughout the 24-year period, 1940–1964, in Puerto Rico. An analysis of the factors which stimulated output growth, capital, and labor will comprise a major segment of the chapter. Specifically, the key question to be answered is what effect did the rapidly improving quality of the labor force have on the output and labor productivity of the economy?

The Growth of the Puerto Rican Economy

The gross commonwealth product of Puerto Rico, a concept identical to the gross national product of the United States, rose from $391,105,000 in 1940 to $1,878,000,000 in 1962 (in real terms, 1957–1959 prices), representing a 6.3 per cent per annum growth rate. Output did not grow smoothly, nor continuously, throughout the 24-year period, 1940–1964. The heavy investment of the United States government in Puerto Rico during World War II stimulated rapid growth of output on the island during the war years. A decrease in output occurred during the immediate postwar years, and the gross commonwealth product did not attain the 1945 level of output until 1948–1949. From 1949, the gross commonwealth product has continued to increase unabated to the present time (1964). The two periods of fastest growth in output occurred during the war, 1940–1945, and the last ten years, 1954–1964.

The prime factor stimulating the growth during the 1940–1945 period was the large-scale investment of the United States government in military bases and factories for the production of wartime goods. A conservative estimate of the military government expenditures on the island was approximately 25 per cent of the gross product. The growth rate of the economy was 9.2 per cent per annum, the highest in the entire 24-year period. The large role of the government can be detected by the rapid rate of growth of output originating in the government sector, 15.3 per cent per annum, which was the fastest growth rate of any of the sectors in the economy during the 1940–1945 period. The large expenditures by the government probably stimulated the growth of all the other sectors, particularly manufacturing, which achieved an impressive 12.9 per cent growth rate per annum.

Extracting the rapid growth of the economy during the war years, the growth rate for the entire postwar period was significant: 5.7 per cent per annum. The leading growth sector during the postwar period was the construction industry, which grew at a rate of 12.8

TABLE 6.1

RATES OF GROWTH OF OUTPUT OF THE PUERTO RICAN ECONOMY
AND ITS COMPONENT SECTORS FOR SELECTED PERIODS

(*Percentages*)

Sectors	1940–1945	1940–1950	1950–1960	1940–1961	1946–1961
Economy	9.2	7.2	6.6	6.3	5.7
Agriculture	7.4	4.8	0.1	2.2	0.6
Manufacturing	12.9	10.7	10.6	9.7	7.4
Construction	—7.8	8.4	10.2	8.5	12.8
Transportation	1.5	6.4	9.1	7.1	7.6
Trade	8.6	12.0	5.7	8.0	5.7
Finance	4.8	5.0	9.8	5.2	9.2
Government	15.3	0.6	7.9	3.9	3.0
Services	7.6	5.1	9.8	5.3	8.6

The output of each sector was converted into real terms by adjusting to a 1957-1959 price base.

Sources: United Nations, Department of Economic and Social Affairs, *National Income Statistics, 1938–1948* (New York: United Nations, 1948) and United Nations, Department of Economic and Social Affairs, *Yearbook of National Accounts Statistics,* 1956 and 1962 (New York: United Nations, 1956, 1962).

per cent per annum. Table 6.1 contains the growth rates for the economy and its component sectors for selected periods of time. Next to the rapid growth of the construction sector, the tertiary component of the economy, finance and services, grew most rapidly, 9.2 per cent and 8.6 per cent, respectively. The manufacturing sector continued to grow at an impressive rate, 7.6 per cent per annum, throughout the postwar period, 1946–1961. The most significant change between the war and postwar growth among the sectors of the economy occurred in the agricultural sector, where the high growth rate of output, 7.4 per cent per annum, during the war years dropped sharply to a negligible growth of 0.6 per cent per annum during the 1946–1961 period.[2]

The stagnation of the dominant sector of a traditional economy would normally result in a deteriorating economic situation, especially with a rapidly growing population. Fortunately for Puerto Rico, the shifting of the composition of output and the rapid growth of the secondary and tertiary sectors of the economy more than compensated for the lack of growth of output in the agricultural sector. The transportation sector experienced the most significant positive change in the growth of output from a low 1.5 per cent per annum growth rate in 1940–1945 to a 7.6 per cent per annum growth rate in the postwar period. Apparently the shortage of materials for transportation construction, cars and roads, and so on retarded the wartime growth of this sector. The postwar expanding economy with rising incomes and the availability of materials caused a rapid increase in the growth of this sector. The government sector's output, with the cessation of the war and its return to normal functions, experienced a significant decrease from a high 15.3 per cent growth rate in 1940–1945 to a 3.0 per cent growth rate in the postwar period.

The period of slowest growth of output occurred during the early postwar years. The growth rate for 1945–1949 was an insignificant

[2] The rate of growth of the output of the agricultural sector was almost identical to the rate of growth of population during the 1950–1960 period. The agricultural output was dominated by one crop, sugar, which was the major export item of Puerto Rico. Puerto Rico was dependent on large importation of food to feed its growing population. The failure of the agricultural sector to expand would have had a serious negative effect on the Puerto Rican balance of payments if emigration did not occur. The growing population without emigration would have increased the demand for greater food imports, and without increased agricultural output to export, the deterioration of the balance of payments would have hurt the economy. In this sense, emigration aided the economic growth of Puerto Rico.

0.35 per cent per annum compared to the growth rate for 1950–1960 of 6.6 per cent and for the entire postwar period of 5.7 per cent per annum. This comparison is somewhat misleading because of the drop in output from the 1945 level during wartime to the significantly lower peacetime level in 1946. (See Table 6.3 for the specific output data for the period 1940–1962.) The rate calculated for the 1946–1949 period is approximately 3.5 per cent per annum, which indicates the economy was not stagnating during the postwar period of 1946–1949 but was growing at a significantly lower rate than in the subsequent periods. Column 4 in Table 6.1 indicates the different rates of growth of the sectors of the economy for the decade 1950–1960. With the exception of the agricultural and trade sectors, every other sector experienced impressive growth rates. The manufacturing sector experienced the highest growth rate during this period, 10.6 per cent per annum. The output of the agricultural sector did not experience any growth in the 1950–1960 period.[3]

A better perspective of the rapid transformation of the Puerto Rican economy can be obtained from the percentage of total income originating in each of the sectors of the economy. Table 6.2 contains the percentages of total income originating in each sector for selected years during the period 1940–1961. The striking transformation of the economy from a traditional agricultural economy into a growing industrial and diversified economy can be seen from the comparison of the 1940 and 1960 percentages of total output originating in each of the sectors. The agricultural and government sector in 1940 accounted for approximately 50 per cent of the total output. Their proportion decreased significantly during the 20-year period and in 1960 they contributed only 25 per cent

---

[3] It should be recognized that while the growth of output was negligible in the agricultural sector, the quantity produced did not decrease and furthermore was produced with a rapidly decreasing labor supply. As a result, labor productivity, that is, output per worker, increased significantly from .52 in 1940 to 1.48 in 1962. This indicates that (a) labor was redundant and disguised unemployment pervaded the sector and as farm laborers emigrated to cities or the United States the remaining workers could be more productive and/or (b) capital-intensive methods and equipment were introduced, causing technological displacement of workers, which stimulated their internal and external migration. In either case, it seems clear that excess labor existed in the sector and the emigration of these workers did not cause output to decrease but had a favorable effect on labor productivity. A more detailed study of the agricultural sector and disguised unemployment in Puerto Rico would confirm definitively the effect of the elimination of the redundancy, a study which is beyond the scope of the present one.

TABLE 6.2

PERCENTAGE OF THE TOTAL PUERTO RICAN INCOME ORIGINATING
IN THE SECTORS OF THE ECONOMY FOR SELECTED YEARS

Sectors	1940	1945	1950	1955	1960	1961
Agriculture	28.1	25.4	22.3	16.0	12.4	11.6
Manufacturing	10.5	13.2	14.9	19.4	21.9	22.4
Construction	4.2	1.5	4.8	4.9	6.7	6.9
Transportation	8.1	5.1	7.5	9.8	9.6	9.6
Trade	10.5	10.2	17.1	17.1	15.8	15.6
Finance	8.9	6.7	8.5	11.1	11.6	11.8
Government	20.4	29.5	10.6	11.2	12.1	12.1
Services	8.8	8.0	7.2	7.8	9.7	9.9

The percentages of each sector are a function of both price and output.
Accurate data on price changes of output for each sector were not available.
Sources: Same as Table 6.1.

to the total output of the Puerto Rican economy. Again the greatest
percentage change among the individual sectors occurred in agriculture, which decreased from 28.1 per cent in 1940 to 11.6 per cent
in 1962. The only other significant decrease occurred in the government sector, with a fall from a 1940 percentage of 20.4 to 12.1
in 1962.

In contrast to the decreases in the previous two sectors, the
rapid growth of the manufacturing sector enabled it to increase its
percentage of total income significantly, from 10.5 per cent in 1940
to 22.4 per cent in 1962. This increase resulted in the manufacturing
sector being the largest single contributor to the total income of
the economy in 1962, almost equaling the role of agriculture in the
1940 economy. In a short period of twenty years the industrial
manufacturing sector grew sufficiently to dominate the agricultural
sector in the economy. Wholesale and retail trade also increased
significantly, from 10.5 per cent of the total income of the economy
in 1940 to 15.6 per cent in 1962. All other sectors experienced slight
increases in the percentages of total income originating in their
sectors. The result of the rapid growth of the nonagricultural sector
of the economy, particularly manufacturing, has transformed the
economy into a more diversified, productive, and dominately industrial economy, significantly reducing its dependency on sugar.

The specific changes in the percentages of income in each of the
sectors for selected five-year periods reveal considerable variations.
The government sector's percentage of total income between 1940
and 1945 increased the most, rising from 20.4 per cent to 29.5

per cent. Practically all of the other sectors experienced stable or decreasing percentages during the war period. (See column 1 in Table 6.2.) Again those industries most heavily dependent on raw materials — construction and transportation — experienced the largest decreases in percentages of output.

The cessation of wartime activities caused a sharp drop in the income originating in the government sector; by 1950 it had declined to 10.5 per cent. The sector which experienced the most significant increase in the five postwar years, 1945–1950, was the trade sector, rising from 10.2 per cent to 17.1 per cent. This sharp increase, apparently resulted from the rapid increases in income per capita which stimulated increased consumption and perhaps from the ease of entry into this sector.

The 1950–1955 period was characterized by stability in the percentages of income originating in the sectors with the exception of a very sharp increase in manufacturing and a correspondingly sharp decrease in agriculture. The sharp reversal of the contributions of these two sectors clearly marks the rapid and significant transformation of the Puerto Rican economy within a relatively short period of twenty years.

Capital Formation in Puerto Rico

A major factor stimulating the rapid growth of output in Puerto Rico was the large-scale capital formation and productive investment that took place during the 1940–1964 period. Gross domestic fixed investment experienced continuous and significant increases throughout the 1940–1962 period. In 1940 gross fixed domestic investment (hereafter referred to as investment unless otherwise specified) was $34,560,000 or only 8.8 per cent of the gross commonwealth product. Throughout the two decades not only did the absolute amount of investment exceed the previous year's investment but, with the exception of two years, 1951 and 1957, the percentage of investment out of gross product increased rapidly and significantly. Table 6.3 contains the data on gross commonwealth product, gross domestic fixed investment, the percentage of investment out of gross product, and an estimate of the capital stock for the period 1940–1962. The rate of growth of investment for the period 1940–1962 was extremely high, 11.9 per cent per annum. The result of this investment was a growing percentage increase of investment out of gross product, which rose from a low 4.9 per cent in 1946 to an all-time high of 28.1 per cent in 1962. The rate of growth of

TABLE 6.3

OUTPUT, INVESTMENT, AND CAPITAL STOCK IN PUERTO RICO 1940–1962

Year	Gross Domestic Fixed Investment (thousands of dollars)	Gross Commonwealth Product (thousands of dollars)	Percentage of GDFI (1) out of GCP (2)	Estimated Capital Stock (thousands of dollars)
1940	34,560	391,165	8.8	1,309,390
1941	40,287	471,859	8.5	1,346,887
1942	67,088	572,585	11.6	1,409,279
1943	13,892	786,283	1.8	1,422,198
1944	52,035	826,938	6.3	1,479,891
1945	46,138	831,452	5.5	1,522,799
1946	37,500	762,000	4.9	1,565,708
1947	72,324	743,085	9.7	1,600,583
1948	115,400	821,725	14.0	1,667,874
1949	142,216	921,998	15.4	1,775,966
1950	157,728	1,026,100	15.4	1,907,427
1951	174,764	1,305,098	13.4	2,054,114
1952	177,332	1,174,701	15.1	2,219,033
1953	177,997	1,177,963	15.1	2,383,951
1954	208,118	1,187,530	17.5	2,577,501
1955	229,622	1,240,066	18.6	2,791,050
1956	277,713	1,325,742	20.9	3,049,323
1957	286,200	1,448,652	19.7	3,315,489
1958	294,500	1,481,800	19.9	3,589,374
1959	339,452	1,564,918	21.7	3,905,064
1960	344,692	1,609,135	21.4	4,225,628
1961	408,796	1,700,627	24.0	4,605,808
1962	527,700	1,878,000	28.1	5,076,500

The method of estimating the capital stock is described in the text. All dollar values are in real terms, adjusted to a 1957–1959 base.

Sources: Same as Table 6.1.

this percentage of investment out of gross product was 5.1 per cent for the 1940–1962 period and was higher for the 1946–1962 period, 6.6 per cent per annum.

The rapid increases in investment occurred during times when capital productivity experienced both rapid increases and decreases. The growth of capital productivity for the entire 1940–1962 period was negligible, 0.9 per cent per annum. (Table 6.8 contains the annual capital productivity figures.) Capital productivity measured as the average productivity of capital Q/K, at first experienced rapid increases growing at a rate of 6.3 per cent per annum between

1940 and 1951. Thereafter, it decreased rapidly at a rate of 4.6 per cent per annum for the period 1951–1962. Despite the declining capital productivity in recent years, investment grew at a phenomenal rate, 12.4 per cent per annum for the period 1947–1962. Falling average productivity implies falling marginal productivity of capital. Apparently investment in Puerto Rico has not decreased in response to the declining marginal productivity of capital.

As the productivity of capital decreased, labor productivity (measured as the average productivity of labor Q/L) increased rapidly, growing at a rate of 6.3 per cent per annum for the 1940–1962 period. The growth of labor productivity and rising real wages did not retard the growth of profits of business enterprises in Puerto Rico, which grew at a rate of 7.8 per cent for the 1940–1962 period and 6.2 per cent for the postwar period, 1947–1962. The evidence seems to indicate that growing profits stimulated investment and declining productivity of capital did not dampen the incentive to invest in Puerto Rican industries. In addition, net profits after taxes in Puerto Rico were sufficiently higher than in the United States because of the tax concessions offered to enterprises investing in Puerto Rico. In any event, rising real wages did not seem to retard investment on the island.

One potential source of capital formation in Puerto Rico was bank deposits, which grew at a rate of 10.1 per cent per annum for the 1940–1962 period. Bank deposits increased from $76,000,000 in 1940 to $776,000,000 in 1962. A slower growth rate of bank deposits, 6.2 per cent per annum, occurred in the postwar period. The most significant portion of the increase in bank deposits was the rapid growth of private savings, which reflected the increased propensity of the population to save out of the additional incomes. The private savings rate grew from $17,000,000 in 1940 to $219,000,000 in 1962, or 11.1 per cent. For the postwar period 1946–1962, the growth of private savings was less than in the war years, but still a significant 8.8 per cent per annum.

The theoretical discussion in Chapter 2 put forward a hypothesis that the average and marginal propensities to save would increase as per capita income increased and would level off at higher income levels. Table 6.4 contains data on income per capita, private savings, savings per capita, savings per capita as a percentage of income per capita, and a marginal savings per capita rate. The last concept is defined as the change in per capita savings as a percentage of income per capita changes. The calculations indicate

TABLE 6.4

PER CAPITA INCOME AND SAVINGS RATES IN PUERTO RICO 1940–1962

Year	Per Capita Income (in dollars)	Private Savings (in millions)	Savings per Capita	Per Cent of Savings per Capita out of per Capita Income	Per Cent of the Change in Savings per Capita out of per Capita Income Changes
1940	278	17	9.1	3.2	n.a.
1941	316	17	8.9	2.8	—.04
1942	378	17	8.7	2.3	—.03
1943	379	24	12.1	3.2	339.00
1944	445	35	17.4	3.9	7.8
1945	n.a.	45	21.9	n.a.	n.a.
1946	n.a.	n.a.	n.a.	n.a.	n.a.
1947	333	54	25.5	7.6	n.a.
1948	340	50	23.2	6.8	—3.2
1949	375	49	22.4	6.0	—2.4
1950	396	51	23.0	5.8	2.6
1951	415	52	23.4	5.6	2.0
1952	461	60	27.2	5.9	8.4
1953	495	68	31.2	6.3	11.5
1954	503	71	32.3	6.4	14.7
1955	511	77	34.4	6.7	26.4
1956	529	86	38.4	7.3	22.2
1957	544	103	45.7	8.4	48.4
1958	570	129	56.2	9.9	40.4
1959	591	139	59.8	10.1	17.1
1960	630	152	64.4	10.2	11.8
1961	662	169	70.2	10.6	15.0
1962	706	219	89.2	12.6	43.2

Dollar values are in real terms, adjusted to constant 1954 price base.

Source: Commonwealth of Puerto Rico, Office of the Governor, Puerto Rico Planning Board, *Selected Indices of Economic and Social Progress, 1939–1940, 1946–1962* (San Juan, Commonwealth of Puerto Rico, 1962).

that as income per capita increased in Puerto Rico, savings per capita also increased; column 4 contains the percentage of savings per capita out of income per capita. The table indicates that more savings occurred as income per capita increased. In 1940 the percentage of savings per capita out of income per capita was a low 3.2 per cent and it increased throughout the two decades, reaching 12.6 per cent in 1962.

Marginal savings per capita as a percentage of changes in income per capita experienced many more fluctuations in the 1940–1950 period but in the 1950–1960 decade a rapid rate of increase occurred, from a low 2.6 per cent in 1950 to an extremely high percentage of 48.4 per cent in 1957. The percentage declined to 11.8 per cent in 1960; however, in two years it returned to a high figure of 43.2 percent in 1962.

The data seem to support the proposition that savings per capita rose as income per capita increased in the Puerto Rican economy during the period of rapid economic growth. This increased savings per capita provided a larger source of capital formation for potential investment. The growth of savings and financial institutions on the island provided the mechanism by which increased availability of capital could be obtained by growing numbers of domestic and foreign entrepreneurs.

It is interesting to note that significant increases in the per capita savings percentage and marginal savings percentage occurred at the $500 level of income per capita. From 1954 to 1961 the per capita income rose approximately $200, and the percentage of savings per capita out of income per capita increased significantly from 6.3 per cent to 12.6 per cent. In contrast, seven years prior to 1954, that is, in the period 1947–1954, income per capita increased by almost the same amount from $333 to $500; but there was no significant increase in the percentage of savings per capita out of income per capita. The percentage stabilized around the 6 per cent level. A similar phenomenon occurred with the relationship between the marginal savings per capita percentage out of the changes in income per capita at the same $500 level of income per capita. (A comparison of the data in columns 1, 4, and 5 in Table 6.4 indicates the change before and after the $500 per capita income level.)

Apparently this rapid increase in savings per capita provided, in part, additional sources of capital for productive investment for the period 1954–1962. Observing the increases in investment from Table 6.1, column 1, we find investment between 1950–1953 to be quite stable, similar to per capita savings. Thereafter, investment increased rapidly, almost trebling in nine short years, from $177,-997,000 to $527,700,000. Although income per capita rose approximately the same amount during the two periods, savings rates increased rapidly only after the $500 level of per capita income was attained. As soon as the savings per capita increased, a sharp increase in investment occurred, indicating that the higher savings rate did provide a fund of potential capital formation in Puerto Rico.

The role of emigration, therefore, played an important indirect role in stimulating capital formation by allowing gains in output to be translated into gains in income per capita, which stimulated savings per capita throughout the country. Additional benefits of emigration, which contributed to the growth of income per capita, were the incomes of temporary and migratory farm workers and remittances from emigrants to friends and relatives in Puerto Rico.[4]

Taking the liberty of a restrictive and unrealistic assumption, that all the other variables are held constant, *ceteris paribus*, we can estimate that the departure of approximately 33 per cent of the population via emigration had the effect of raising income per capita 33 per cent. Under this assumption, the 1962 level of per capita income ($706) would be reduced by one third, or $235, to a level of $471, or the level of per capita income that existed in 1952–1953. Interestingly, this level of income per capita is below the point where the percentage of savings per capita begins to rise rapidly. Thus the level of income per capita, savings per capita, and hence a part of capital formation that would have prevailed if emigration had not occurred would be comparable to the pre-1953 levels. The great surge in savings per capita, capital forma-

[4] Data on farm earnings of migratory Puerto Rican workers in the United States are not available. An interview with the director of the farm workers' migratory program working in the New York branch of the Department of Migration provided some qualitative information on the income earned by migratory farm workers. Approximately 12,000 to 18,000 farm workers per year work in the United States and return to Puerto Rico after the harvest season. Fortunately, the slack agricultural season in Puerto Rico corresponds to the peak season in the United States. The director estimated that approximately $1,000 per worker were earned. If we assumed that one half was saved, a reasonable amount in light of the nominal costs of room and board, then approximately $6,000,000 to $9,000,000 would be saved and brought back to the island, contributing to the rising income per capita levels.

With regard to personal remittances received by the island population from the emigrants in the United States, it totaled in 1956–1957 $23,000,000 and increased to $34,000,000 in 1960–1961.

Both sources of additional income from the temporary farm migration and the permanent emigration stimulated the growth of income per capita and in turn contributed to the increased domestic savings on the island.

The source of data for the personal remittances was Commonwealth of Puerto Rico, Office of the Governor, Puerto Rican Planning Board, Bureau of Economics and Statistics, *Economic Report to the Governor*, 1961 (San Juan, Commonwealth of Puerto Rico, 1961).

tion, and of course output, which began to grow rapidly in 1953, would just be commencing in 1963. Although the *ceteris paribus* assumption is somewhat unrealistic, it does provide a rough qualitative estimate of the possible benefits derived from large-scale emigration.

Capital Stock of Puerto Rico

The large increase in domestic savings and the profitability of Puerto Rican enterprises stimulated increased capital investment. The result of this was significant growth in the capital stock of Puerto Rico. Precise data on capital stock were unavailable, but an estimate was calculated. The basic assumption was that the average incremental capital-output ratio throughout the twenty-year period 1940–1960[5] was a sufficiently close approximation of the capital-output ratio prevailing in 1940. The average incremental capital-output ratio was 3.6 and was calculated as the sum of each year's incremental ratio (which was gross domestic fixed investment divided by the change in output of the given year) divided by the number of years. This ratio of 3.6 was multiplied by the gross product in Puerto Rico in 1940 to arrive at a capital stock figure of $1,309,990,000 in 1957–1959 prices. Yearly capital stock figures were derived by depreciating the capital stock by an arbitrary 7 per cent per annum and then adding the gross domestic fixed investment to the capital stock for each year.[6] Table 6.3, column 4, contains the estimated annual capital stock for Puerto Rico for the years 1940–1962. The rate of growth of capital stock for this period was 5.9 per cent per annum and for the postwar period it was higher — 7.2 per cent per annum. This rapid rate of capital formation was a major stimulant of increased output, higher capital-labor ratios, and increased output per worker during the 1960–1964 period of rapid economic growth.

[5] The incremental capital-output ratios calculated for the period 1940–1945 were eliminated from the calculation of the average incremental capital-output ratio because of the widespread variations and unusually low figures. The latter was probably due to the unusual investment pattern and the urgency for rapid production during wartime.

[6] The arbitrary selection of 7 per cent depreciation rate was based on two factors, the composition of the capital stock which was approximately 50 per cent each for building and equipment, and an arbitrary assignment of a seven-year length of life on equipment and a twenty-three-year length of life for buildings. The average fifteen-year length of life for capital stock provided a 7 per cent depreciation rate. The rate is probably overstated because of the longer length of life of buildings in a tropical climate.

Income per Capita and Labor Productivity

Emigration of large numbers of unskilled workers had two definite effects on the labor force in Puerto Rico: (1) it increased the dependency proportion of the population and (2) it improved the quality of the labor force by raising the proportion of skilled to unskilled workers in the economy. To avoid negative effects on income as a result of an exodus of workforce members, output per worker (labor productivity) in Puerto Rico had to increase enough to compensate for the increased dependency ratio. The growth of income per capita during the 1940–1964 period was very impressive. The rapid growth of output, described previously, was translated into rapid growth of income per capita due, in part, to large-scale emigration reducing the growth of population.

Unfortunately, available data on output and income per capita in Puerto Rico prior to 1940 are quite spotty and not very reliable. Although it is difficult to assess the specific economic conditions prevailing for each of the years 1930–1940, sufficient evidence in qualitative statements and isolated pieces of statistical data indicate that the economy was not stagnating but, even more serious, was rapidly deteriorating during the 1930–1940 period.

> If the condition of the masses of the Island people in the period before 1928 could be described as "deplorable," then the situation of the Puerto Rican people in the next thirteen years can only be described as bordering on the "critical." Production in most of the major branches of the economy fell, income contracted drastically, a very large proportion of the labor force was unemployed, and most families on the island experienced great distress.[7]

Although population growth was not the cause of the declining economic situation during this period, nevertheless the economy and specifically income per capita did not grow appreciably between the 1929 level of $122 and the 1939 level of $130.[8] The rapid and large capital investment during the war years in Puerto Rico, 1940–1945, stimulated the growth of output to the point where it exceeded the growth of population. In short, a low-level income trap caused by population growth was avoided. Nevertheless, the growth of income per capita was severely retarded by the rapid growth of population during the 1940–1947 period. In 1940 per capita income (1954 prices) was $278, and in 1947 it rose to $333,

[7] Harvey Perloff, *op. cit.*, p. 30.
[8] *Ibid.*, p. 31.

equivalent to a 2.47 per cent per annum growth rate. In contrast, with the occurrence of large-scale emigration, commencing in 1946, the rapid growth of output was almost entirely translated into rapid growth of income per capita. Population growth during the decade of the 1950's averaged only 0.6 per cent per annum. The result of the combination of rapid output growth and large-scale emigration was a growth of income per capita of 4.9 per cent per annum for the 1947–1960 period,[9] as shown in Table 6.5.

TABLE 6.5

PER CAPITA INCOME AND LABOR PRODUCTIVITY GROWTH RATES IN
PUERTO RICO FOR SELECTED INDUSTRIES AND SELECTED PERIODS
(*Percentages*)

	1940–1962 per Annum	1940–1950 per Annum	1950–1960 per Annum	1954–1962 per Annum
Per Capita Income	4.3	4.0	4.9	
Labor Productivity				
Economy	6.0	6.2	6.7	6.1
Agriculture	4.5	5.6	5.3	4.4
Manufacturing	7.7	10.9	5.6	6.9
Commerce	5.3	5.4	5.4	4.1

Sources: Data used for the growth rate calculations taken from United Nations, Department of Economic and Social Affairs, *Yearbook of National Accounts Statistics,* 1956 and 1962, and *National Income Statistics 1938–1948* (New York: United Nations, 1948, 1956, 1962).

Note: The growth rates are in real terms, adjusting income and output to a 1957–1959 base.

Since the percentage of employed workers out of the total population fourteen and over decreased, the rapid rate of growth of income per capita implies even more rapid rates of growth of output per worker, that is, labor productivity. The actual growth of the labor force during the period under study was negligible. The rapid growth of capital stock during the same period of time caused significant and rapid rates of growth of the capital-labor ratio which directly affected labor productivity in Puerto Rico. The capital-labor ratio grew at a rate of 5.4 per cent per annum

[9] For comparative purposes, Puerto Rico had one of the highest growth rates of income per capita in the world. Only Germany (8.4), Japan (7.4), and Israel (5.6) exceeded the Puerto Rican rate of 5.1. In contrast, the United States grew at 1.6, Canada at 1.3, and Mexico at 1.4 during the same period of time, 1950–1960. Commonwealth of Puerto Rico, Office of the Governor, Puerto Rican Planning Board, Bureau of Economics and Statistics, *Economic Report to the Governor,* 1963 (San Juan, Commonwealth of Puerto Rico, 1964), p. 2.

for the 1940–1962 period. The highest growth rate in the capital-labor ratio occurred during the last twelve years, 1951–1962, a rate of 8.3 per cent per annum. Labor productivity for the economy, measured in terms of national income at factor cost divided by man-years of labor, grew at a rate of 6.3 per cent per annum for the 1940–1962 period. This rate was sufficient to compensate for the increased dependency of the population and also to result in rapid growth of income per capita. Table 6.6 shows the yearly capital-

TABLE 6.6

LABOR PRODUCTIVITY OF SELECTED INDUSTRIES IN THE PUERTO RICAN
ECONOMY AND THE ECONOMY'S CAPITAL-LABOR RATIO*

Year	Agriculture	Manufac- turing	Commerce	Economy	Capital/ Labor
1940	.52	.80	.83	.79	2.44
1949	.86	2.17	1.46	1.30	2.82
1950	.91	2.39	1.66	1.47	3.03
1951	1.12	2.39	1.53	1.60	3.13
1952	1.00	2.68	1.63	1.73	3.97
1953	1.08	2.60	1.88	1.80	4.39
1954	.99	2.52	1.96	1.82	4.82
1955	1.08	3.24	2.11	2.04	5.06
1956	1.07	3.32	2.24	2.11	5.55
1957	1.11	3.10	2.30	2.22	6.03
1958	1.17	3.38	2.37	2.40	6.52
1959	1.36	3.92	2.59	2.66	7.18
1960	1.54	4.19	2.52	2.86	7.61
1961	1.46	4.50	2.80	2.99	9.05
1962	1.48	4.68	2.84	3.14	8.47

Sources: Output data same source as Table 6.1 and also Commonwealth of Puerto Rico, Office of the Governor, Puerto Rico Planning Board, Selected Indices of Economic and Social Progress, 1939–1940, 1947–1962 (San Juan, Commonwealth of Puerto Rico, 1962). Employment data from Commonwealth of Puerto Rico, Department of Labor, Bureau of Labor Statistics, Earnings and Employment (San Juan, Commonwealth of Puerto Rico, 1952–1962).
* Labor productivity was calculated by dividing the national income at factor cost by man-years of labor.

labor ratios and the labor productivity of the economy and three industries — agriculture, manufacturing, and commerce — for the period 1940–1962. Labor productivity grew most rapidly during the 1950–1960 period: 6.7 per cent per annum. Labor productivity in manufacturing was the highest, growing at a rate of 7.7 per cent per annum for the entire period.

A markedly higher labor productivity growth rate was attained in the manufacturing sector during the 1940–1950 decade in contrast to the subsequent decade. There is some evidence indicating that recent capital investment in the manufacturing sector is channeled into less labor-intensive industries. The introduction of capital equipment in labor-intensive handicraft home industries of textiles and clothing may account for a large part of the greater labor productivity in this sector during the 1940–1950 period. An examination of recent rates of growth of labor productivity for the period 1954–1963 indicates that the manufacturing sector had greater growth rates and higher productivity than the two other sectors — agriculture and commence — and for the entire economy. (See Table 6.5.) Although capital-labor ratio data for individual sectors were not available, usually the manufacturing sector has higher capital-labor ratios and would account for the higher labor productivity and the faster growth rates compared to the other sectors of the economy. As for the economy's labor productivity (which increased 125 per cent during the 1948–1962 period), it appears that the 200 per cent increase in the capital-labor ratio during the same period was a contributing factor.

Effects of Labor Quality on Output and Productivity

Introduction

The importance of the growth of capital stock in stimulating the growth of output in Puerto Rico should not be underestimated. On the other hand, while the growth of the labor force was negligible, the quality of labor (defined as the proportion of skilled to unskilled workers) changed significantly. The specific objective of this section is to arrive at an estimate of the effect of the improvements in the quality of the labor force on the growth of output. Knowledge of the effect of the quality of labor on the growth of output can provide a basis for evaluating the effect of emigration. But more significantly, the contribution of quality of labor to output growth can be used to evaluate the economic benefits of investment in education, which played a major role in developing the quality of the labor force.

The literature on human capital, investment in education, and its effect on economic growth has grown rapidly in the past five years. Professor Schultz started the exploration, and others such as Solow, Kendrick, Dennison, Domar, Harbison, and Myers have continued to analyze the area of technological progress and the effect of education and human capital on economic growth.[10] Most of the recent works have been directed at measuring technological progress or the residual after labor and capital inputs have accounted for their share in the growth of total productivity. The focus here will be on examining the effect of changes in labor quality on the growth of output. The methodology employed accounts for portions of technological progress that are embodied in the capital and adjusted labor inputs.

The problem of estimating the effect of an improved quality of the labor force on output is complicated by many factors too numerous to mention specifically. Three factors presenting particular difficulty here were (1) the limitations of available data for industries and for the economy with respect to capital and labor inputs; (2) the difficulty of isolating the interdependency between capital and labor, especially in industries with fixed proportions prevailing; and (3) the possibility that additional variables not included in the analysis as well as external economies may be at the center of the contributions to output that are attributed to the two inputs of capital and labor in the production function.

In light of the numerous obstacles strewn across the researcher's path, a different approach was used to discover whether labor, in its constant quest for improvement through education, training, and experience, has contributed to the growth of output. The methodology consisted of estimating a Cobb-Douglas production function for the Puerto Rican economy with two inputs — capital and labor, the latter adjusted for quality changes. The coefficients were not restricted to equal one. The regression of the dependent output on capital and labor provided the coefficients of each of

[10] Theodore W. Schultz, "Investment in Human Capital," *American Economic Review*, Vol. LI, No. 1 (March 1961), p. 3; Robert M. Solow, "Technical Change and the Aggregate Production Function," *Review of Economics and Statistics*, Vol. XXXIV, No. 3 (August 1957), p. 312; John W. Kendrick, *Productivity Trends in the United States* (Princeton, N.J.: Princeton University Press, 1961); Evsey Domar, "On the Measurement of Technological Change," *Economic Journal*, Vol. 71, No. 284 (December 1961), p. 709; Edward F. Dennison, *The Sources of Economic Growth in the United States and the Alternatives before Us*, Supplementary Paper No. 13 (New York: Committee for Economic Development, 1962); Frederick Harbison and Charles A. Myers, *Education, Manpower and Economic Growth: Strategies of Human Resource Development* (New York: McGraw-Hill Book Co., 1964).

This is by no means an exhaustive list of the literature on this subject of education, investment in human capital and economic growth, and technological progress, but it does represent the different approaches used to understand the complex relationships involved in this subject.

the two inputs. With the coefficient of labor available from the production function estimate, an estimate of the output of Puerto Rico was obtained by substituting raw labor — that is, unadjusted for quality — in the production function with the same capital input and coefficients. In this manner, the differences between the actual output and the estimated output would indicate the contribution that the quality of the labor force made to output in Puerto Rico.

A similar method with a variation was used to estimate the changes in quality of labor on the growth of output. An estimate of output was obtained by starting with a stock of quality labor in a base year and instead of adding skilled or quality labor inputs, substituting unskilled labor inputs. The same coefficients for capital and labor were used in the estimate. In other words, starting from a specified year with the capital and labor quality stocks given, what would the difference in output be when raw or unskilled labor was substituted in the production function? The difference between the actual and estimated output in the terminal year would be attributed to the changes in the quality of the labor force during the period.

Data

The estimation procedure for the capital stock of Puerto Rico was described in a previous section.[11] Both the capital and output data were adjusted to constant prices, 1957–1959 base. The output data used were gross commonwealth product.

The labor force data and the changes in quality based on changes in occupational composition of the labor force were described in Chapter 4. Unfortunately, specific occupational data for years prior to 1952 were not available, and consequently the time series used

---

[11] The estimate of the 1940 capital stock is arbitrary and subject to error, but it will not seriously change the estimation of the effects of improved quality of labor on the growth of output. The major reason is that the analysis begins in 1952 and only a small percentage of the capital stock of 1940 is available during the 1952–1962 period.

The depreciation rate of 7 per cent is probably too high, thus understating the size of the capital stock. Nevertheless, it would not result in a significant reduction of the size of the contribution of quality of labor on the growth of output for the following reasons: (a) a lower depreciation rate (2 per cent) would not have a significant effect on the magnitude of capital stock; (b) the profile path of investment was heavily weighted in the later period, thus minimizing the effect of a high depreciation rate during the earlier years; (c) the size of the labor coefficient swamped the capital coefficient so that it would take very large increases in the capital stock to affect the size of the estimates significantly.

to estimate the production function was confined to the 1952–1962 period. It would have been desirable to calculate the effect of labor quality on specific industries' output, but capital and occupational labor distribution were not available.

Labor inputs were adjusted for quality in the following manner: (1) it was assumed that the real wage equals the marginal productivity of labor in each occupation; (2) a calculation of the occupational wage ratios was used as the weight for each occupation[12] (that is, if the wage ratio of craftsmen was four times that of farm laborers, then each craftsman would be equal to four farm laborers); (3) each occupational ratio was multiplied by the number of people engaged in each occupation for a given year. The summation of all the people in each occupation adjusted by the wage ratio weight gives the total labor inputs adjusted for quality.[13]

Data on yearly variations in hours worked were not available, but a further quality refinement was attempted by using a constant yearly man-hour weight based on different hours worked per year by various occupations. The weight was based on occupational man-hours which were calculated for the two census years 1950 and 1960. From this calculation, arbitrary approximations of man-hours worked were assigned to the various occupations in the following manner: unskilled laborers, 1,200 hours per year; semiskilled workers, 1,400 hours per year; skilled workers, 1,600 per year; and professional and managerial manpower, 1,800 hours per year.[14] It

[12] Data on occupational wage ratios can be found in Chapter 5. The range of weights attached to occupations from professional workers to unskilled workers was 4.75 in 1952 to 4.18 in 1962. The range for skilled workers was 2.5 to 2.2 for 1952–1962. For semiskilled workers, the range was 1.6 to 1.7.

[13] Kendrick, *op. cit.* In his comprehensive productivity study Kendrick weighted the man-hour inputs by the average hourly earnings in each industry of the economy in order to obtain aggregate measure of labor input. My method of weighting by the ratio of occupational earnings provides a more refined attempt at estimating the quality of the labor inputs used in the production of goods and services throughout the economy. An analysis of sectoral output and productivity would require the occupational composition of labor by industry and industry occupational wage data. If Kendrick's average hourly earnings data were derived by a weighted average of the wages of each subclass of labor in the industry times the number of laborers in each subclass, then the two weighting systems should yield similar results in estimating the effect of quality of labor on the growth of output.

[14] The occupations were subdivided into different skill classifications as follows: the professional category included managers, owners, and officials, and technical, semiprofessional, and professional occupations; the skilled category included craftsmen, foremen, and kindred occupations; the semiskilled classification included operatives, sales, clerical, and service occupations; and the unskilled category included laborers, farm laborers, and domestic workers.

is important to note that this weighting of quality by man-hours does not reflect actual variations in yearly man-hours worked in Puerto Rico. In short, it is a constant quality weighting for each year, compared to the man-year labor quality adjustment. The reason for using both types of adjusted inputs is that the use of man-years probably gives a better indication of the benefit of improved labor quality;[15] but since man-hours data on a yearly basis do not exist, the man-hours estimate is not a legitimate man-hours labor input used in most labor productivity studies. Thus, one input provides a better indication of productivity, while the other provides a better indication of labor quality used in producing the economy's output. Appendix C contains the adjusted and unadjusted labor inputs for the 1952–1962 period.

Estimation and Results

The production function fitted to the Puerto Rican economy was a Cobb-Douglas type of the following form:

$$Q = C \ L^*a, \ K^b \qquad (6.1)$$

where Q equals output, $C = $ a constant, a and b are coefficients of labor and capital, respectively, and L^* represents labor adjusted for quality, and K represents capital stock. In order to treat the coefficients as elasticities with respect to output, the production function was placed in logarithmic form:

$$\log Q = C + a \ \log L^* + b \ \log K \qquad (6.2)$$

The data on output, capital stock, and labor adjusted for quality of labor inputs in terms of man-years for the ten-year period, 1952–1962 yielded the following estimates of the input coefficients:

$$\log Q = -2.6 + .93385 \ L^*, \ .36445 \ K \qquad (6.3a)$$
$$(.274) \qquad (.068)$$

The R corrected for degrees of freedom was .9929 and the corre-

---

[15] This method of weighting labor inputs is invariant to aggregation. In order to weight the system in this way, it is necessary to use wage rates for classes of labor that are calculated by a weighted average of the wage of each subclass of labor times the number of laborers in each subclass. This allows each subclass to be subdivided into more classes of labor, but the sum total would still be equal to the total wage bill of labor.

Symbolically:

Given: $W_1 L_1 + W_2 L_2 = WL$

If: $L_1 = L_a + L_b, \ L_2 = L_c + L_d, \ W_1 = W_a L_a + W_b L_b / L_a + L_b, \ W_2 = W_c L_c + W_d L_d / L_c + L_d$

Then: $W_a L_a + W_b L_b + W_c L_c + W_d L_d = W_1 L_1 + W_2 L_2 = WL$

sponding R^2 was .9858. The standard errors of the coefficients (placed in parentheses) were both insignificant. Partial correlation coefficients of the two inputs were $L^* = .768$ and $K = .883$. The excellent fit of the regression equation indicates that practically all of the output changes were explained by the input changes of capital and quality of labor. The elasticities when converted into shares for labor and capital turn out similar to the United States estimates; for Puerto Rico it was 72 per cent labor and 28 per cent capital shares. The Durbin-Watson statistic was 2.38, sufficiently close to the desirable 2.00 to dismiss the occurrence of serial correlation.[16]

The production function estimated with man-hours adjusted for quality of labor yielded the following results:

$$\log Q = -2.2 + .88285 \ L^{**} + .4113 \ K \qquad (6.3b)$$
$$(.230) \qquad\quad (.049)$$

with an R corrected for degrees of freedom of .994 and an R^2 of .988. The partial correlation coefficient of labor was .804 and capital was .946. Serial correlation was absent as indicated by the Durbin-Watson statistic of 2.37. The calculations of the shares of the inputs from the elasticities were also similar to the United States estimates: labor was 67 per cent and capital 33 per cent in Puerto Rico.

Given the elasticities (coefficients) of the two measures of adjusted labor inputs, the raw labor inputs were multiplied by these labor coefficients and added to the same capital stock and capital coefficient in the original production function. The estimated output with raw labor substituted for quality labor is presented in Table 6.7, along with the actual output in Puerto Rico. Symbolically the difference between the actual output Q and the estimated output Q^1 represents the effect of the quality of the labor force in the two production functions:

$$\log Q = C + a \ \log \ L^* + b \log \ K \qquad (6.2)$$
$$\text{and}$$
$$\log Q^1 = C + a \ \log \ \bar{L} + b \log \ K \qquad (6.2a)$$

---

[16] The absence of serial correlation can be observed from the alternating signs of the residual terms in the regression analysis. The alternation of signs indicates that the expected and actual output did not run parallel throughout the period under study.

TABLE 6.7
ACTUAL AND ESTIMATED OUTPUT IN PUERTO RICO WITH LABOR
ADJUSTED AND UNADJUSTED FOR QUALITY
(In dollars)

Year	Actual Output	Estimated Output with Raw Labor (in man-hours)	Estimated Output with Raw Labor (in man-years)	Estimated Output with Raw Labor Inputs after 1952 (in man-hours)	Estimated Output with Raw Labor Inputs after 1952 (in man-years)
1952	1,175	615	670	1,175	1,175
1953	1,178	615	682	1,187	1,190
1954	1,187	624	694	1,206	1,216
1955	1,240	660	737	1,235	1,269
1956	1,326	689	772	1,295	1,318
1957	1,449	701	815	1,335	1,350
1958	1,482	723	816	1,350	1,390
1959	1,565	738	837	1,425	1,437
1960	1,609	774	880	1,468	1,482
1961	1,701	821	937	1,541	1,551
1962	1,878	889	1,015	1,620	1,643

The actual labor inputs raw and adjusted for quality are in Appendix 3. Columns 4 and 5 contain quality adjusted labor stock for 1952, but all labor inputs after 1952 are unadjusted for quality of labor, that is, raw labor.

All dollar terms are in thousands.

where the same capital stock and coefficient appear in both production functions holding the effect of capital constant, but L^* and $\bar{L}$ represent quality labor and raw labor, respectively.

The results of the actual and estimated output with different labor inputs are interesting and striking. The man-years estimate, which contains a lower quality of labor adjustment, had a higher output estimate than the man-hours adjustment. The closer outputs between estimated output with man-years and actual output are expected since the labor inputs are closer to each other than the man-hours estimate. The man-hours estimate of output was 10–15 per cent below the man-years estimate of output for the eleven-year period. Man-years estimated output was 57.8 per cent of actual output in 1952 and 54.0 per cent in 1962; for man-hours, estimated output was 52.3 per cent of actual output in 1952 and 47.3 per cent in 1962. The decreasing percentage indicates that the more rapid increases in the quality of labor at the end of the time period increased the differential between actual and estimated output.

The results of the analysis are significant: *approximately 42–46 per cent of the output can be attributed to quality of labor inputs in terms of man-years and 48–53 per cent of total output in terms of man-hours.* The growth of the quality of the Puerto Rican labor force, and not its size, combined with the growth of capital stock to explain the significant proportion of the growth of output in Puerto Rico. The large investment in education in Puerto Rico, rising from $6.4 million in 1940, or 1.3 per cent of GCP, to $96 million in 1962, or 5 per cent of GCP,[17] contributed significantly to the growth and improvement in the quality of the Puerto Rican labor force. Apparently, this decision to improve its major resource — its people — had a direct benefit in increasing the size of total output by 40–50 per cent of the level it would have attained with capital investment if the labor force had consisted of unskilled farm laborers.

The second method consisted of attempting to estimate what effect the actual changes in the quality of labor at a given point in time had on the actual growth of output during the same period of time. The base year was 1952, where the output, capital, and labor adjusted for quality and their respective coefficients were used for the estimation of the output resulting from labor quality changes. Unskilled labor inputs were used instead of skilled labor inputs and were added to the stock of existing quality labor in 1952.

The last two columns in Table 6.7 contain the estimated output resulting from the changes in labor quality since 1952. The smaller output estimate again corresponds to the labor input in terms of man-hours. The comparison of the actual and estimated output due to quality changes indicates that the growth of quality of labor accounted for approximately $259 million in output in terms of man-hours, or 14 per cent more than would have been produced

[17] William H. Knowles, "High-Level Manpower in Puerto Rico," *Education and Manpower: Country Studies in Economic Growth*, eds., Frederick Harbison and Charles Myers (New York: McGraw-Hill Book Co., 1964). The growth of education in Puerto Rico has been quite rapid; for example, in 1940 only 10,000 students were enrolled in high school compared to approximately 200,000 in 1962. The effect of this increased education on the future quality of the labor force will be quite significant. A calculation of the costs and benefits of the expenditure on education would be an interesting and informative study.

during the 1952–1962 period. In terms of man-years, it would have been $236 million, or approximately 13 per cent. More significantly, the difference in the change in actual output was $703 million from 1952–1962. The percentage of this change in output because of quality of labor adjustment was 37 per cent and 34 per cent in terms of man-hours and man-years, respectively. In other words, *more than one third of the growth of output during the last ten years was attributed to the rapidly improving quality of the labor force.* The fact that emigration withdrew a greater proportion of unskilled to skilled labor than existed in the Puerto Rican labor force and thus upgraded the skill composition indicates that it played a part in stimulating the growth of output. The return flow of skilled emigrants, which raised the level of skill in the labor force, and the improved educational facilities for the smaller population after emigration both had a positive effect on the skill level of the labor force and in turn on the growth of output. Thus, the redundancy of the Puerto Rican farm labor force[18] and the departure of these workers did not have a negative effect on output; on the contrary, it raised the quality of the labor force in the economy.

Clearly, the two sets of estimates indicate that the quality of the labor force and the changes over time in Puerto Rico had a significant impact on the growth of output during the 1952–1962 period. Since the quality of the labor force changed considerably between 1940 and 1952, even greater influence on the growth of output would be found if data were available to undertake the specific calculations.

The proposition that it was increased capital investment that caused the skill development of the labor force is not very persuasive in light of the requirement of a long gestation period in the educational process to raise the occupational distribution. A more reasonable proposition is that the growth of the skilled labor force in Puerto Rico was probably an important factor in attracting for-

[18] Accurate information and detailed studies of disguised unemployment in Puerto Rico were not available. An estimate of the amount of disguised unemployment was one third of the labor force in agriculture during the late 1940's. The source was the Agricultural Extension Service, associated with the Department of Agricultural Economics at the University of Puerto Rico, Rio Piedras, Puerto Rico. The maintenance of output levels without a declining labor supply supports the contention of large-scale disguised unemployment in this sector.

eign investment there, especially in modern technologically complex industries requiring skill and manpower to operate the equipment efficiently.[19]

An attempt to estimate the proportion of labor productivity attributable to the quality of the labor force was undertaken with the use of the adjusted labor inputs. The calculations of labor productivity, defined as the national income divided by labor inputs in man-years and man-hours, both adjusted for quality and unadjusted are presented in Table 6.8. The output per worker, regardless of the type of labor input, rose appreciably throughout the 1948–1962 period. The calculations of labor productivity using the adjusted quality labor inputs indicate that almost half of the gain in labor productivity resulted from the improved quality of labor.

Specifically, the difference in output per worker with adjusted and unadjusted labor inputs in terms of man-years was 44 per cent in 1948 and increased to 50 per cent in 1962. In terms of man-hours, adjusted and unadjusted, the difference attributed to quality of labor in the economy's labor productivity was 47 per cent in 1948 and 55 per cent in 1962. The labor productivity figures ad-

---

[19] The external economies derived from an educated, flexible, and mobile labor force should not be ignored or underestimated for underdeveloped economies. This is especially important with regard to locational decisions for new plants. Industries and firms operating under semifixed or fixed factor proportions will consider the level of the skills of the labor supply a crucial determinant in the decision to locate new plants. With regard to fixity of factors of production, particularly with modern, complex, capital-intensive equipment, an inherent psychological rigidity may operate to overlook the possibilities of other techniques of production.

Despite the existence of significantly lower prices for the abundant factor of production, managers may not adjust their techniques merely to follow the strict dictates of economic theory and maximize their profits. The psychological rigidity against operating under modern conditions and techniques in which they are most knowledgeable and trained will retard the transformation to more profitable methods of production. The employment of labor-intensive technologies to benefit from the abundant factor implies retrogression back to old-fashioned technology and a loss of status.

If this proposition is valid and firms do not adjust to factor prices, restrained not by technology but by this psychological rigidity, the importance of a skilled labor force is more vital in order to entice new investments in plants. The close relationship of Puerto Rico with United States investments in new plants on the island, rather than only a flow of capital to the country, makes the importance of a skilled labor force crucial for the attraction of new plants. Many firms with fixed proportions necessary or perceived necessary to continue operations would find it profitable to operate in Puerto Rico under the generous tax concessions; but if a skilled labor force did not exist they would not be able to invest in the island.

TABLE 6.8

LABOR PRODUCTIVITY WITH LABOR INPUTS ADJUSTED AND UNADJUSTED
FOR QUALITY AND CAPITAL PRODUCTIVITY IN PUERTO RICO

Year	Output per Raw Labor Input (in man-hours)	Output per Adj. Labor Input (in man-hours)	Percentages, Column 2/1	Output per Raw Labor Input (in man-years)	Output per Adj. Labor Input (in man-years)	Percentages, Column 4/3	Output per Capital Input
1948	1.39	.78	.56	.99	.52	.53	.49
1949	1.50	.83	.55	1.07	.55	.51	.52
1950	1.63	.92	.56	1.16	.58	.50	.54
1951	1.99	1.07	.54	1.42	.71	.50	.64
1952	2.10	1.13	.54	1.50	.76	.51	.53
1953	2.17	1.17	.54	1.55	.78	.50	.49
1954	2.22	1.22	.55	1.59	.80	.50	.46
1955	2.25	1.21	.54	1.61	.79	.49	.44
1956	2.38	1.27	.53	1.70	.83	.49	.43
1957	2.64	1.36	.52	1.88	.88	.47	.44
1958	2.69	1.37	.51	1.92	.89	.46	.41
1959	2.87	1.45	.50	2.06	.93	.45	.40
1960	2.90	1.46	.50	2.07	.94	.45	.38
1961	2.97	1.48	.50	2.12	.96	.45	.37
1962	3.13	1.57	.50	2.24	1.02	.45	.37
Percentage Change 1948–1962	125	101		126	96		—24

Sources: All calculations were from data cited in earlier tables.

justed for quality show an approximate 25 per cent smaller increase compared to the unadjusted labor productivity figures for the period 1948–1962 for both man-years and man-hours estimates.

In conclusion, it is probable that more than half of the measured labor productivity in the Puerto Rican economy can be attributed to the quality of the labor force for the period 1948–1962. Most likely the other 50 per cent can probably be attributed to the rising capital-labor ratio.

Summary

The data presented in this chapter provide a clear picture of the rapid growth and changes that occurred in the Puerto Rican economy during the past twenty-four years. The transformation of a stagnating, one-crop sugar economy into a dynamic, diversified, progressive industrialized economy within the short period of two decades was a remarkable achievement. The economy experienced rapid rates of growth of output, income per capita, and labor productivity. The large quantities of capital invested in physical and human resources by both private and public parties was a significant cause of the rapid growth of the economy.

The decision of the Puerto Rican government to invest immediately large sums of capital in the most valuable natural resource on the island — its people — through education and training was important in bringing about an improved quality of the labor force. The quality of the labor force contributed significantly to the growth of output and productivity throughout the two decades. Emigration also played a significant role in reducing the population growth, eliminating redundant workers, and raising the skill composition of the labor force. The effect of emigration was to stimulate the rate of growth of income per capita which, in turn, led to increased savings and greater capital investment during the period of economic change on the island of Puerto Rico.

Thus, the combined effect of large-scale emigration and considerable physical and human capital investment was sufficient to enable the economy to be transformed into a dynamic, growing economy, providing impressive increases in the standard of living of the population.

Summary and Conclusions

The preceding chapters have analyzed, empirically and theoretically, the effects of emigration on the economic growth of an underdeveloped, densely populated country. The theoretical analysis explored the potential beneficial effect of emigration on the economic growth of a country that experiences rapid population growth and significant amounts of disguised unemployment in the agricultural sectors as well as open unemployment in the industrial sector of the economy. In order for emigration to have a substantial effect on economic growth, two conditions were found to be essential: (a) the size of the emigration must be sufficient to affect significantly the rate of population growth; and (b) the migrants must be unskilled, uneducated, and for the most part redundant workers.

The theoretical analysis contained several crucial hypotheses that, if empirically valid, would mean that emigration had a significant positive effect on the economic growth of Puerto Rico. The three major hypotheses were (a) that the birth rate is an inverse function of per capita income during the stage of rapid economic growth; (b) that the savings rate is a positive and increasing function of the income per capita level during the early stages of economic growth; and (c) that occupational composition of the migrants is a function of the absolute and relative earnings differentials between two areas.

The empirical analysis of the Puerto Rican emigration supports the validity of these hypotheses. The first section of this chapter contains a summary of the major findings on the effect of emigration on crucial components of the Puerto Rican economy. The final section discusses the implications of migration for the future eco-

157

nomic growth of Puerto Rico and its usefulness for other less developed nations.

During the past two decades, Puerto Rico experienced rapid and sustained economic growth. Output grew at a rate of 6.3 per cent per annum, one of the highest growth rates in the world. During this period of rapid economic development, a large mass emigration of Puerto Ricans to the United States occurred. The evidence presented in the preceding chapters indicated that the Puerto Rican emigration played an important role in the remarkable economic growth of the island.

Prior to 1940, the economy of Puerto Rico was stagnating, with a constant per capita income of approximately $100. The economy was completely dependent on a major agricultural export commodity, sugar. The existence of significant disguised unemployment in agriculture and open unemployment throughout the economy and the use of backward, traditional techniques and equipment plagued the economy. Population was growing at a rate of 2.0 per cent per annum, and the future prospects of raising the standard of living on the island were quite poor.

Fortunately, the outbreak of the Second World War stimulated considerable United States investment in Puerto Rico, specifically for the wartime production effort. This burst of capital investment was a major factor in moving the economy from a position of stagnation toward the path of successful economic development.

At the same time that the economy experienced its first measurable economic growth in recent years, another phenomenon — a demographic revolution — was occurring that threatened to absorb the gains of economic progress. Puerto Rico experienced a dramatic decline in the death rate, in part because of large-scale government expenditures in the area of public health. This, coupled with a slight rise in the birth rate, caused significant increases in the growth of population between 1940 and 1947. The rate of growth of population during these seven years increased from 2 per cent to 3 per cent per annum, a 50 per cent increase. This change represented a marked structural shift from the population growth rates of the past forty years, which averaged approximately 1.7 per cent per annum. The rapid rate of population increase absorbed a considerable portion of the gains in output growth during the 1940–1947 period, thus preventing the rapid growth of income per capita. However, output growth was sufficient to outweigh the growth of population, thereby avoiding stagnation and a constant income per capita. Nevertheless, while the growth of output was a very high 5.5 per cent per annum, income per capita grew at a significantly lower rate of 2.4 per cent per annum.

At the time when rapid population increases threatened the rate of future growth of the Puerto Rican economy, large-scale emigration of Puerto Ricans to the United States commenced in 1945 and 1946. The size of the migration was substantial compared to the population on the island, averaging almost 50,000 people annually or approximately 2 per cent of the population per year during the period 1950–1960. The total postwar emigration amounted to 600,-000. With the addition of the children born to the Puerto Rican migrants in the United States, the total number of Puerto Ricans residing in the United States in 1960 reached 900,000. This figure represents 38 per cent of the current population of 2,400,000 living on the island today. The migration stream reached its peak during the early 1950's and has declined significantly during the past three years, 1960–1963, averaging under 10,000 per annum.

Puerto Rican emigration had its most significant impact on the size and growth of the island population. The estimated rate of population growth, under the assumption of no emigration and a prevailing high fertility rate, would have been 3.5 per cent per annum during 1950–1960. Instead, emigration converted the rapid rate of natural increase, over 3 per cent in 1947, into a negligible population growth of 0.6 per cent per annum during the 1950–1960 period. The estimated population of the island would have been 3,700,000 people in 1963, or 1,300,000 additional people residing on a poor, densely populated island. This represents 53 per cent more people than are currently living on the island of Puerto Rico. The findings indicate that emigration was the major factor contributing to the reduction of the expected rate of population growth of 3.3 per cent per annum to 1.2 per cent per annum during the two decades 1940–1960, a reduction of 67 per cent.

The control of population growth by large-scale emigration had a significant impact on the rate of growth of per capita income. While this grew at a rate of 2.4 per cent prior to 1947, during the period of emigration (1947–1962) per capita income increased at a rate of approximately 5.0 per cent per annum. The considerable reduction of the rate of population growth allowed a larger proportion of the gains from the growth of output to be directly converted into substantial improvements in the level of per capita income of the Puerto Rican people. The importance of these rapid changes in the standard of living and in the economic environment on the attitudinal and behavioral aspects of the population should not be underestimated as necessary conditions for the stimulation of future economic growth.

The statistical evidence clearly indicates that emigration had an important impact on the reduction of the present size and growth of the population. Moreover, emigration had a significant effect on the age structure and thus on the future growth of the population. The examination of the characteristics of the migrants revealed that 85 per cent of the migrant population were in the age bracket 15–44, which includes the bulk of the reproductive members of the population. The departure of these people caused a 34 per cent reduction in the number of people in the 15–44-year-old group on the island. One of the immediate results was the decline in the birth rate after only a short seven-year time lag from the fall in the death rate in 1940. The smaller base of the population pyramid caused by the reduction in births, the hollowing of the present reproductive population by emigration, and the slight increase in the number of people over sixty years of age via immigration caused a substantial change in the age structure of the population that will reduce the future rate of population growth in the decades to come.

In the last few years several factors have been responsible for the reduction in size of the migration stream: (1) the narrowing of earnings differentials between the United States and Puerto Rico; (2) the reduction in the strength of push factors as income per capita and standards of living have improved in Puerto Rico; (3) the reduction of disguised unemployment in Puerto Rico; (4) the return of significant numbers of migrants, particularly the more skilled workers. With the decreased size of the migration stream and the existence of very low death rates, the changes in the birth rate will be the major determinant of the future population growth of Puerto Rico. Since 1947 the birth rate fell considerably, from 44 to 30 per thousand. Nevertheless, the rate of natural increase of the population was quite high, 2.4 per cent in 1963. Rapid population growth in the 1960's without large-scale emigration may be a severe handicap to the future economic growth of the island. This problem has caused considerable concern and alarm on the part of the leaders of Puerto Rico.

A calculation of annual fertility rates indicated that a marked decrease (10 per cent) occurred during the 1950–1960 period. The regression analysis and cross-section data indicated that income per capita and education were the two major factors associated with the declining birth and fertility rates in Puerto Rico. This tends to point to an optimistic future with regard to the direction of the future birth rate trend in Puerto Rico. The future growth of population will be determined, in part, by the rate of growth of the economy, particularly by the improvements in education and income per capita available to the population.

The emigration of a large segment of the population aged 15–44 affected the size of the Puerto Rican labor force significantly. Although capital investment and output increased rapidly during the twenty years, 1940–1960, the labor force increased by only 20,000 workers. The migration stream contained a considerably higher proportion of labor force members than the proportion on the island. In 1960, 297,000 out of 617,000 emigrants, or 48 per cent, were labor force members. The result of emigration was a substantial reduction in the size of the labor force from 705,000 in 1950 to 625,000 in 1960. In recent years, 1960–1963, the size of the migration stream has decreased sharply and at the same time the labor force has expanded to 675,000.

The migrant population had a much higher labor force participation rate than the island population, 48 per cent to 31 per cent, respectively. The female migrants had the greatest differences in labor force participation rates for all age categories. The bulk of the male and female migrants were labor force members in the age bracket 15–24. The movement of these workers was a major factor in the reduction of the Puerto Rican labor force participation rates from 32 per cent in 1940 to 25 per cent in 1960.

Emigration reduced the potential size of the Puerto Rican labor force by almost 50 per cent. That is, if all Puerto Ricans in the United States labor force remained in the Puerto Rican labor force, an additional 325,000 workers would be in the 1963 labor force. This would raise the size of the Puerto Rican labor force to 1,000,-000 workers. However, even though emigration reduced the size of the labor force, this decrease was not sufficient to lower the measured rate of unemployment on the island, which averaged 13 per cent for the two decades. Nevertheless, emigration most likely succeeded in reducing the observed present rate of unemployment from what it would have been if emigration had not occurred. Despite large amounts of capital investment, the amount of employment generation was not sufficient to reduce the unemployment, even though the labor force did not grow significantly.

However, the investment and emigration combined probably contributed to the reduction of disguised unemployment and underemployment in the economy. Clearly, if emigration had not occurred, the expansion of the labor force and the lack of employment generating capital would have resulted in considerably higher measured rates of unemployment, increased disguised unemployment in agricultural and retail trading sectors and general underemployment throughout the economy. An estimate of the magnitude of potential unemployment without emigration was in the range of 25–33 per cent of the projected labor force. The consequences of such a high rate of unemployment are difficult to ascertain, but it seems probable that with rising aspirations and higher educational attainment of the new entrants into the labor force, a high rate of unemployment would have been intolerable. Increased frustrations of a vocal and active segment of the society might have led to sufficient pressures to change the political, social, and economic structure of Puerto Rico. Instead of a show place of development and democracy with rising standards of living, the island might have turned into a shameful poorhouse of hunger, misery, poverty, and dictatorship.

The large numbers of labor force members who emigrated resulted in population increases exceeding the increases of the labor force, which caused an increased dependency ratio of the population. However, the postwar emigration was predominantly a family-type movement and the dependency ratio did not increase significantly. The percentage of productive to nonproductive population — that is, the employed labor force out of the total population — decreased from 27 per cent to 25 per cent in the two decades. The fact that the labor force participation rates decreased more than the above ratio, indicated that many of the migrants were either unemployed or were replaced by other workers and machinery. It is possible that an increased dependency ratio of a population can often lead to decreases in the income per capita level of the economy. In the case of Puerto Rico, labor productivity increased considerably and not only offset the increased dependency ratio but stimulated significant increases in the growth of per capita income. Labor productivity grew at an impressive 6.7 per cent per annum during the 1950–1960 decade, accounting for the 5 per cent growth rate of income per capita.

During this period of rapid economic growth, the occupational distribution of the Puerto Rican labor force underwent significant changes. The labor force was considerably upgraded and improved by (a) the large amounts of capital invested in formal education and training; (b) the increased demand for skilled labor, stimulated by large capital investments; and (c) large-scale emigration. The most significant changes occurred in the growth of the skilled worker classifications, particularly professional, managerial, and craftsmen. In contrast, the most significant decreases occurred among the agricultural occupations of farm laborers, foremen, and farmers. These changes in the occupational distribution of the labor force reflect the basic underlying changes of the sectors within the economy. Puerto Rico was transformed into a diversified, dynamic industrialized economy within the short time span of twenty years. The result of this transformation and the investment in education and training was a significant increase of the skilled proportion of the labor force, rising from 13 per cent in 1940 to 26 per cent in 1960. Over the same period the unskilled proportion decreased from 39 per cent in 1940 to 26 per cent in 1960.

Emigration had a definite impact on the quality of the Puerto Rican labor force. A study of the occupational characteristics of the migrants indicated that a greater proportion of unskilled workers was in the migrant stream than the proportion in the Puerto Rican population. The higher unskilled to skilled worker ratio among the migrants resulted in an upgrading of the labor force in Puerto Rico. Emigration did not result in an increased supply of skilled personnel, which occurred only in the last three years, but it removed the unskilled and redundant laborers and indirectly reduced the pressure on the educational system; thus it allowed new entrants into the labor force to obtain higher educational levels on the island.

The movement of unskilled migrants changed the unskilled to skilled ratio on the island considerably. The ratio was 4.9 for the migrants in 1950 compared to the expected ratio, assuming no emigration, of 3.5 on the island. The differences in the unskilled to skilled ratio widened between 1950 and 1960. In 1960 the ratio for the migrants was 5.7 compared to the expected ratio of 2.7 on the island. The result of emigration and education caused the unskilled to skilled ratio of workers on the island to decrease significantly from 5.0 to 2.1 during the period 1940–1960. The change in the ratio caused by emigration was slightly more than 50 per cent of the total change, or slightly higher than the change through education. In short, emigration played an important role in changing the unskilled to skilled ratio directly by the emigration of unskilled workers and by the return flow of skilled workers in recent years. Emigration also contributed indirectly to raising the educational attainment of the population remaining on the island by easing the pressure of educating a substantial number of school-age children who emigrated with their parents or who would have been born in Puerto Rico.

The changing composition of the occupations of the migrant population was associated with and determined, in part, by the absolute and relative occupational earnings differentials between Puerto Rico and the United States. It was hypothesized that once a minimum income per capita level was attained by the population, those who had the greatest incentive to emigrate in terms of relative and absolute occupational earnings differentials would emigrate in the greatest proportion. The data seem to support this hypothesis. The greatest earnings differential between Puerto Rico and the mainland was for the unskilled workers, particularly farm laborers, and these workers migrated in the greatest proportion once their income was sufficient to bear the immediate costs of migration. The smallest differential in earnings existed between skilled professional occupations and they were the smallest proportion of the migrant population. In fact, the recent trend of skilled manpower back to Puerto Rico indicated that the relatively favorable position for skilled workers in Puerto Rico was sufficient to compensate for their decreased absolute earnings.

An examination of the differential unemployment rates by occupations in Puerto Rico and New York City indicated that the occupational unemployment rates in New York were higher than in Puerto Rico in 1950 and almost identical in 1960. In addition, an examination of the unemployment rate in Puerto Rico and for Puerto Ricans in the United States indicated that the latter rate exceeded the former in 1950 and 1960. Apparently, migrants were not moving in response to job vacancies, unless Puerto Ricans do not consider unemployment rates of fellow Puerto Ricans and/or their occupations and merely respond to the general level of unemployment in the United States. Since it is more likely that the information regarding employment for Puerto Ricans came from other migrants, whose experiences tend to be confined to other Puerto Ricans and to more specific occupations, there are serious doubts that Puerto Ricans respond to general unemployment levels. Thus it appears that the Puerto Rican emigrants continued to migrate despite poorer employment opportunities because the significant earnings differentials were sufficient to compensate for the higher unemployment of Puerto Ricans in the United States.

The analysis of the effect of the quality of the labor force on output and labor productivity in Puerto Rico indicated that (a) approximately 50 per cent of output and labor productivity was attributed to the quality of the labor force and (b) the improvement in the quality of the labor force from 1952 to 1962 accounted for 35 per cent of the growth of output during the same period.

The major findings summarized in this chapter indicate that Puerto Rican emigration considerably benefited the variables strategic to economic growth on the island in the past twenty years:

1. Substantial portions of the rapid growth of output and labor productivity can be attributed to the improved quality of the labor force, which was favorably affected by emigration.

2. Emigration effectively reduced the size and growth of the population and the labor force. The result was rapid increases in income per capita levels and the standard of living of the people on the island.

3. Emigration raised the labor-land ratio and the capital-labor ratio in the agricultural sector and the capital-labor ratio and the skilled labor to unskilled labor ratios in the nonagricultural sectors of the economy. The higher capital-labor and skilled labor-unskilled labor ratios had a favorable effect on the increased labor productivity in all of the sectors of the economy, most notably in manufacturing.

4. The significant increases in output per worker more than compensated for the slight increase in the dependency proportion of the population. The result was a rapid growth of income per capita, which stimulated increased savings and contributed to higher capital formation and productive investment.

5. Although real wages increased, capital investment continued to grow throughout the period in response to higher profits before and after taxes.

6. The existence of open and disguised unemployment on the island prevented labor shortages despite the large-scale emigration. In fact, emigration reduced the amount of disguised unemployment in agriculture and underemployment in the economy, which brought reductions in government expenditures for welfare and relief payments and allowed for increased government investment in productive "Fomento" projects.

The gains in per capita income and the reduction of unemployment were determined, in part, by the large-scale emigration. Today, the population of the island enjoys the highest income per capita level, $710, in Latin America. Emigration was a crucial variable in the success story of economic growth and prosperity of Puerto Rico.

Implications for the Future Economic Growth of Puerto Rico

The negligible size of the emigration stream during the 1960's leaves Puerto Rico with a rate of population growth of 2.5 per cent in 1963. The active role of the Catholic Church against birth control techniques makes the population problem even more difficult. With rapid population growth, gains in income per capita will be more difficult to attain, and this will delay the favorable effect that higher income has in reducing the birth rate. There are two major policy areas through which the government can help solve the population problem of the 1960's. The allocation of money to increase the educational attainment of the population is an important policy variable. The objective of the government to provide twelve grades of education to every child, if accomplished, should have a crucial effect on reducing the future birth rate. The importance of 8–12 grades of education, particularly for females, as an effective means of reducing fertility on the island requires that an additional priority of government funds should be given to elementary and secondary education. The initiative in recent years to establish and increase the number of rural schools on the island will aid in the reduction of the future birth rate. The rural areas with the highest birth rates are in greatest need of more education to cope with the problems of an industrializing society. Puerto Rico's future prosperity depends on the development of its richest natural resource — its people. A sound elementary and secondary education will provide the people with the attitudes, knowledge, and ability to contribute to a more productive and prosperous economy.

Education also contributes to the significant improvement in the quality of the labor force. A fundamental education prepares workers for more complex and difficult tasks in a rapidly changing industrialized economy. The analysis indicated the importance of an improving labor force in the past growth of the Puerto Rican economy: future growth will be even more dependent on the rapid development of the labor force. Therefore, the Puerto Rican government, with aid from the United States government, should continue to invest significant amounts of capital in the educational system of Puerto Rico.

Although a cost and benefit analysis of the returns from various levels of education was not undertaken, it is the author's opinion that greater attention should be given to the development of elementary and secondary education. Exchange programs with the colleges and universities in the United States should be examined for the future development of Puerto Rican professional manpower. In addition, more attention should be given to vocational education and on-the-job training for the many technical skills needed by modern industries. Improved quality of the secondary and higher educational systems may be needed in order to meet the higher skill requirements of technologically changing industries. In general, a re-evaluation of the educational system in accordance with the future manpower needs may be necessary for the stimulation of the future economic growth of Puerto Rico.

The other policy area under government control is emigration. Additional efforts to stimulate emigration may be desirable, especially if population growth and unemployment emerge in the future. Better information regarding housing, employment, and wages for migrants would be beneficial. A more active and larger role on the part of the United States government in aiding the migrants with retraining and adjustment to a new environment, better schools, and special language instruction are all needed. In light of the war on poverty program, the problems and needs of the Puerto Rican migrants should deserve serious attention.. The more difficult adjustment of farm laborers residing in a large urban area increases the need for better programs to ease the hardship and cost to the individual migrant and the community.

The Broader Applicability of the Puerto Rican Experience

Although emigration was a significant and beneficial factor in the economic growth of Puerto Rico, it is not safe to generalize that it will be useful for all underdeveloped countries desiring rapid economic growth. There are several reasons.

First of all, despite the gains derived from emigration, it is not a cost-free phenomenon. The society incurred the costs of raising and educating the departing population without receiving a direct measurable return for its investment. Indirectly, their mobility may be a return from their education, for without the awareness of other alternatives, emigration may not have occurred. On the other hand, while the society incurred the costs of maintaining the population, if the prospects of obtaining productive employment for these people are poor, then the absence of emigration would require the society to continue to support the population without any future returns. If the problem is lack of education and training to fill the jobs available, then it would probably be beneficial to consider retraining these people. If the problem is long-run redundancy and these people can find employment and better wages in other areas, it is economically beneficial to their country for them to emigrate. Since the bulk of the migrants would be unskilled and redundant, the costs of emigration would be minimized and the gains would be sufficiently greater than the costs, resulting in a net gain from emigration.

Second, emigration can play a positive part in the economic development of countries that possess economic characteristics similar to those of Puerto Rico, excluding the relationship with the United States (that is, countries with disguised unemployment in agriculture and an excess supply of labor in the industrial sector), if unskilled and redundant labor emigrate. Many Caribbean islands and Central American countries have conditions quite similar to those existing in Puerto Rico prior to 1945. The opportunity for migration to the less populated countries of South America without a language and cultural barrier should be examined and perhaps emigration stimulated to aid the economic growth and improve the standard of living of these densely populated countries. The size of the effective migration would be relatively small from these sending countries in relation to the size of the receiving countries, for example, Brazil, which possesses considerable amounts of land and natural resources. A better distribution of population and resources might result in an improved standard of living for the migrants and greater economic growth for both the sending and receiving countries. In light of the beneficial aspects of emigration for the less developed, densely populated countries, the possible benefits of immigration for the sparsely populated and more developed economies such as Australia and Brazil should be re-examined. In addition, the significance of aiding these less developed countries to raise their standards of living should stimulate many advanced and uncrowded countries such as the United States to analyze the costs of a more liberal immigration policy.

Finally, it is important to recognize that many other factors played a significant role in the spectacular economic growth of Puerto Rico. Large-scale foreign investment from the United States; free mobility of the factors of production, especially labor; the absence of defense expenditure; the substantial amounts of federal aid from the United States; the effort of the industrial development company under government auspices; the significant investment in education and the development of an improving quality of the labor force; the excellent and determined leadership; the close association with the United States markets — all were important contributors to the development of a poor agricultural economy into a growing, dynamic, prosperous industrializing economy.

Despite the above differences, every effort and technique should be examined and, if found beneficial, employed in the task of raising the levels of living throughout the world. This study indicates that emigration can have a decisive effect on the economic growth of underdeveloped, densely populated countries — providing the proper conditions exist and other means are employed in conjunction with emigration to develop these economies.

Appendices

NET MIGRATION OUT OF PUERTO RICO 1910–1962

Period	Net Migration
1910–1919	11,000
1920–1929	42,000
1930–1939	18,000
1940	400
1941	600
1942	1,700
1943	3,200
1944	11,200
1945	13,600
1946	39,900
1947	24,600
1948	32,800
1949	25,700
1950	34,700
1951	52,900
1952	59,100
1953	69,100
1954	21,500
1955	45,500
1956	52,300
1957	37,700
1958	27,700
1959	30,000
1960	16,300
1961	7,800
1962	10,800

Source: United States Department of Justice and the San Juan Office of Immigration and Naturalization Service.

APPENDIX B

DATA ON INDEPENDENT AND DEPENDENT VARIABLES IN THE REGRESSION ANALYSIS OF BIRTH AND FERTILITY PATTERNS

Year	Birth Rate	Fertility Rate	Enrollment in Junior and Senior High School Projected 5 Years (in thousands)	Female Labor Force Participation Rate	Percentage of Agricultural Employment out of Total Employment	Per Capita Income Lagged One Year (in dollars) 1940 Base	1960 Base	Population 15–44 Estimated	Ratio of Skilled to Unskilled Labor
1947	43.2	95.8	36	25.9	39.9	197	333	955,000	20.4
1948	40.8	91.1	62	26.5	38.4	264	340	963,000	21.3
1949	39.2	89.5	64	25.5	37.0	261	375	956,000	21.7
1950	38.5	89.7	78	27.4	36.2	291	396	952,000	22.6
1951	37.8	87.8	86	28.6	33.6	315	415	956,000	23.4
1952	36.4	84.1	97	28.2	33.6	323	461	953,000	23.3
1953	35.5	82.3	98	26.8	31.3	352	495	940,000	23.7
1954	35.5	82.0	99	27.2	32.2	369	503	951,000	23.3
1955	35.4	83.9	104	26.7	30.4	377	511	944,000	25.5
1956	34.9	84.3	113	26.3	28.8	386	529	932,000	27.5
1957	33.8	82.0	117	25.6	27.5	405	544	927,000	29.8
1958	33.2	80.8	130	25.9	27.2	413	570	942,000	31.0
1959	32.3	78.4	140	25.7	25.1	418	591	955,000	32.0
1960	32.2	77.7	153	27.2	23.1	437	630	978,000	33.1
1961	31.4	74.2	166	27.9	23.7	452	662	1,018,000	35.9

Sources: Birth rate from Commonwealth of Puerto Rico, Department of Health. All other data from the Commonwealth of Puerto Rico, Office of the Governor, Puerto Rico Planning Board, *Historical Statistics 1959* and *Selected Indices of Economic and Social Progress, 1939–1940, 1947–1962* (San Juan, Commonwealth of Puerto Rico, 1960, 1962).

APPENDIX C

LABOR INPUTS ADJUSTED AND UNADJUSTED FOR QUALITY
IN PUERTO RICO 1952–1962

Year	Man Years Unadjusted (in thousands)	Man Hours Unadjusted (in millions)	Man Years Adjusted (in thousands)	Man Hours Adjusted (in millions)
1952	559	782	1,032	1,547
1953	543	760	1,005	1,516
1954	534	748	973	1,473
1955	551	771	1,023	1,565
1956	557	780	1,046	1,602
1957	549	769	1,066	1,640
1958	550	770	1,081	1,667
1959	544	762	1,082	1,674
1960	555	777	1,104	1,709
1961	572	801	1,147	1,779
1962	599	839	1,193	1,844

Source: Unadjusted labor inputs from Commonwealth of Puerto Rico, Department of Labor, Bureau of Labor Statistics, *Employment and Earnings*, 1952–1962 quarterly and annual reports (San Juan, Commonwealth of Puerto Rico, 1952–1962).

Adjustment of labor for quality is described in the text.

Bibliographic Entries

BOOKS AND MONOGRAPHS

Agarwala, A. N., and S. P. Singh, eds. *The Economics of Underdevelopment*. New York: Oxford University Press, 1963.

American Assembly, Columbia University. *The Population Dilemma*. Englewood Cliffs, N.J.: Prentice-Hall, Inc., 1963.

Baer, Werner. *The Puerto Rican Economy and United States Economic Fluctuations*. Rio Piedras: University of Puerto Rico, Social Science Research Center, 1962.

Baum, Samuel. *Population, Manpower, and Economic Development of Eastern Europe*. Washington, D. C.: Population Research Project, George Washington University, 1961.

Chenault, Lawrence R. *The Puerto Rican Migrant in New York City*. New York: Columbia University Press, 1938.

Coale, Ansley J., and Edgar M. Hoover. *Population Growth and Economic Development in Low Income Countries: A Case Study of India's Prospects*. Princeton, N.J.: Princeton University Press, 1958.

Cochran, Thomas C. *The Puerto Rican Businessman: A Study in Cultural Change*. Philadelphia: University of Pennsylvania Press, 1959.

Creamer, Daniel, and Henrietta L. Creamer. *Gross Product of Puerto Rico 1940-1944*. Rio Piedras: University of Puerto Rico, Social Science Research Center, 1948.

Davison, R. B. *West Indian Migrants*. London: Oxford University Press, 1962.

Dennison, Edward. *The Sources of Economic Growth in the United States and the Alternatives Before Us* (Supplementary Paper No. 13). New York: Committee for Economic Development, 1962.

Descartes, S. L. *Basic Statistics on Puerto Rico*. Washington, D. C.: Office of Puerto Rico, 1946.

Enke, Stephen. *Economics for Development*. Englewood Cliffs, N.J.: Prentice-Hall, Inc., 1963.

Fairchild, Henry Pratt. *People: The Quantity and Quality of Population*. New York: Henry Holt, 1939.

173

Friedman, Milton. *A Theory of the Consumption Function.* Princeton, N.J.: Princeton University Press, 1957.

Geisert, Harold L. *Population Problems in Mexico and Central America.* Washington, D. C.: Population Research Project, George Washington University, 1959.

Hancock, Ralph. *Puerto Rico, A Success Story.* Princeton, N.J.: Van Nostrand, 1960.

Handlin, Oscar. *The Newcomers: Negroes and Puerto Ricans in a Changing Metropolis.* Cambridge, Mass.: Harvard University Press, 1959.

Harbison, Frederick, and Charles A. Myers. *Education, Manpower, and Economic Growth: Strategies of Human Resource Development.* New York: McGraw-Hill Book Co., 1964.

Higgins, Benjamin. *Economic Development.* New York: W. W. Norton and Company, Inc., 1959.

International Labour Office. *International Migration, 1945–1957.* Geneva: La Tribune de Genève, 1959.

Isaac, Julius. *Economics of Migration.* London: Kegan Paul, Trench, Trubner and Company, 1947.

Jaffe, A. J. *People, Jobs and Economic Development.* Glencoe, Ill.: The Free Press, 1959.

Kendrick, John W. *Productivity Trends in the United States.* Princeton, N.J.: Princeton University Press, 1961.

Knowles, William H. "High Level Manpower in Puerto Rico," *Education and Manpower: Country Studies in Economic Growth.* Edited by Frederick Harbison and Charles A. Myers. New York: McGraw-Hill Book Co., 1964.

Lebergott, Stanley. *Manpower in Economic Growth: The American Record Since 1800.* New York: McGraw-Hill Book Co., 1964.

Leibenstein, Harvey. *Economic Backwardness and Economic Growth.* New York: John Wiley & Sons, Inc., 1957.

Mills, C. Wright, Clarence Senior, and Rose Kohn Goldsen. *The Puerto Rican Journey.* New York: Harper and Brothers, 1950.

Myers, Charles, and George Shultz. *The Dynamics of a Labor Market.* New York: Prentice-Hall, Inc., 1951.

National Bureau of Economic Research. *Demographic and Economic Change in Developed Countries.* Princeton, N.J.: Princeton University Press, 1960.

Nurkse, Ragnar. *Problems of Capital Formation in Underdeveloped Countries.* Oxford: Oxford University Press, 1953.

Osborn, Fairfield, ed. *Our Crowded Planet*. London: George Allen and Unwin, 1963.

Perloff, Harvey S. *Puerto Rico's Economic Future*. Chicago, Ill.: University of Chicago Press, 1950.

Rand, Christopher. *The Puerto Ricans*. New York: Oxford University Press, 1958.

Reynolds, Lloyd George. *The Structure of Labor Markets, Wage and Labor Mobility in Theory and Practice*. New York: Harper and Brothers, 1951.

Ruiz, Paquita. *Vocational Needs of Puerto Rican Migrants*. Rio Piedras: University of Puerto Rico, Social Science Research Center, 1947.

Sauvy, Alfred. *Fertility and Survival*. New York: Criterion Books, Inc., 1961.

Senior, Clarence. *Puerto Rican Emigration*. Rio Piedras: University of Puerto Rico, Social Science Research Center, 1947.
————. *Strangers Then Neighbors—from Pilgrims to Puerto Ricans*. New York: Freedom Books, 1961.

Smith, Kenneth. *The Malthusian Controversy*. London: Routledge and Kegan Paul, 1951.

Spengler, Joseph J., and Otis Dudley Duncan, eds. *Population Theory and Policy*. Glencoe, Ill.: The Free Press, 1956.

Stead, William H. *Fomento—The Economic Development of Puerto Rico*. Washington, D. C.: National Planning Association, Pamphlet 103, 1958.

Steward, Julian H. *The People of Puerto Rico: A Study in Social Anthropology*. Urbana, Ill.: University of Illinois Press, 1956.

Taft, Donald R., and Richard Robbins. *International Migrations: The Immigrant in the Modern World*. New York: Ronald Press Co., 1955.

Thomas, Brinley, ed. *Economics of International Migration*. New York: St. Martin's Press, Inc., 1958.
————. *Migration and Economic Growth*. London: University Press of Cambridge, 1954.

United Nations, Department of Economic and Social Affairs. *National Income Statistics, 1938–48*. New York: United Nations, 1948.
————. Population Studies No. 28. *The Future Growth of the World Population*. New York: United Nations, 1958.
————. Population Studies No. 27. *Recent Trends in Fertility in Industrialized Countries*. New York: United Nations, 1958.
————. *Economic Characteristics of International Migrants: Statistics*

for Selected Countries, 1918–7945. New York: United Nations, 1956.

————. *Yearbook of National Statistics, 1956, 1962.* New York: United Nations, 1962.

United Nations, Department of Social Affairs, Population Division. *The Determinants and Consequences of Population Trends.* New York: United Nations, 1953.

ARTICLES

Adelman, Irma. "An Econometric Analysis of Population Growth," *American Economic Review,* Vol. LIII, No. 3 (June 1963), pp. 314–339.

Domar, Evsey. "On the Measurement of Technological Change," *Economic Journal,* Vol. 71, No. 284 (December 1961), pp. 709–729.

Eckaus, Richard S. "Factor Proportions in Underdeveloped Countries," *American Economic Review,* Vol. XLV (September 1955), pp. 539–565.

Fei, John C. H., and Gustav Ranis. "Innovation, Capital Accumulation and Economic Development," *American Economic Review,* Vol. LIII (June 1963), pp. 283–313.

Fleisher, Belton. "Some Economic Aspects of Puerto Rican Migration," *Review of Economics and Statistics,* Vol. XLV (August 1963), pp. 245–253.

Galenson, Walter, and Harvey Leibenstein. "Investment Criteria, Productivity and Economic Development," *Quarterly Journal of Economics,* Vol. LXIX (1955), pp. 343–369.

Hagen, Everett E. "Population and Economic Growth, *American Economic Review,* Vol. XLIV, No. 3 (June 1959), pp. 310–327.

Lewis, Arthur W. "Economic Development with Unlimited Supplies of Labor," *The Manchester School of Economics and Social Studies,* Vol. XXII (May 1954), pp. 139–191.

Nelson, R. R. "A Theory of the Low-Level Equilibrium Trap," *American Economic Review,* Vol. XLVI, No. 5 (December 1956), pp. 894–908.

Reder, Melvin. "The Economic Consequences of Increased Immigration," *Review of Economics and Statistics,* Vol. XLV, No. 3 (August 1963), pp. 221–230.

Rosenstein-Rodan, Paul N. "Notes on the Theory of the Big Push." Cambridge, Mass.: Massachusetts Institute of Technology, Center of International Studies, 1957.

————. "Problems of Industrialization of Eastern and South-Eastern Europe," *Economic Journal,* Vol. LIII (June 1943), pp. 202–211.

Schultz, Theodore W. "Investment in Human Capital," *American Economic Review,* Vol. LI, No. 1 (March 1961), pp. 1–17.

Solow, Robert. "A Contribution to the Theory of Economic Growth," *Quarterly Journal of Economics,* Vol. LXX, No. 1 (February 1956), pp. 65–91.

————. "Technical Change and the Aggregate Production Function," *Review of Economics and Statistics,* Vol. XXXIV, No. 3 (August 1957), pp. 312–320.

GOVERNMENT PUBLICATIONS

Commonwealth of Puerto Rico, Committee on Human Resources. *Unemployment, Family Income and Level of Living in Puerto Rico.* San Juan: Commonwealth of Puerto Rico, 1959.

Commonwealth of Puerto Rico, Department of Agriculture, Bureau of Agricultural Statistics. *Facts and Figures on Puerto Rico's Agriculture 1963.* Santurce, 1963.

Commonwealth of Puerto Rico, Department of Health. *Bulletin of Vital Statistics 1940–1962.* San Juan, Commonwealth of Puerto Rico, 1962.

Commonwealth of Puerto Rico, Department of Health, Division of Demographic Registry. *Annual Vital Statistics Report—1962.* San Juan, Commonwealth of Puerto Rico, 1962.

Commonwealth of Puerto Rico, Department of Labor, Bureau of Employment Security, Committee on Human Resources. *Puerto Rico's Manpower Needs and Supply.* San Juan, Commonwealth of Puerto Rico, 1957.

Commonwealth of Puerto Rico, Bureau of Labor Statistics. *Characteristics of Passengers Who Traveled by Air Between Puerto Rico and the U.S.* San Juan, Commonwealth of Puerto Rico, 1957–1962.

————. *Employment, Hours and Earnings in Puerto Rico.* San Juan, Commonwealth of Puerto Rico, 1952–1962.

Commonwealth of Puerto Rico Fourth Legislative Assembly, Joint Committee of Socio-Economic Research. *Population Changes Outside the San Juan Metropolitan Area.* San Juan, Commonwealth of Puerto Rico, 1960.

Commonwealth of Puerto Rico, Office of the Governor, Puerto Rican Planning Board, Bureau of Economics and Statistics. *Comparative Statistics of the San Juan Metropolitan Area.* San Juan, Commonwealth of Puerto Rico, 1961.

————. *Economic Report to the Governor 1961*. San Juan, Commonwealth of Puerto Rico, 1962.

————. *Economic Report to the Governor 1963*. San Juan, Commonwealth of Puerto Rico, 1964.

————. *Income and Product, Puerto Rico, 1940, 1947–1960*. San Juan, Commonwealth of Puerto Rico, 1964.

————. *Selected Indices of Social and Economic Progress*. San Juan, Commonwealth of Puerto Rico, 1962.

————. *Statistical Yearbook—Historical Statistics*. San Juan, Commonwealth of Puerto Rico, 1959.

New York State Commission for Human Rights, Division of Research. *The Puerto Rican Population of the New York City Area*. New York, May 1962.

United States Department of Commerce, Bureau of the Census. *U.S. Census of Population: 1960*, Final Report PC(11-53A). Washington, D. C.: United States Government Printing Office, 1961.

————. *Census of Population: 1950, Characteristics of the Population*, Parts 51–54. Vol. II. Washington, D. C.: United States Government Printing Office, 1961.

————. *Census of Population: 1960, Characteristics of the Population, Puerto Rico*. Washington, D. C.: United States Government Printing Office, 1961.

————. *Census of Population: 1950, Puerto Ricans in the Continental United States, 1950*. Washington, D. C.: United States Government Printing Office, 1953.

————. *Census of Population: 1960, Puerto Ricans in the United States*. Washington, D. C.: United States Government Printing Office, 1963.

United States Department of Labor, Bureau of Labor Statistics. Special Regional Report, Middle Atlantic Regional Office, New York, 1962. *Employment, Earnings and Wages in New York City*. Washington, D. C.: United States Government Printing Office, 1960.

————. *Occupational Wage Survey*, Bulletin Series 1000+. Washington, D. C.: United States Government Printing Office, 1952–1962.

————. "The Status of Labor in Puerto Rico, Alaska, Hawaii," *Monthly Labor Review*. Bulletin No. 1191 (January 1956), pp. 1–99.

UNPUBLISHED MATERIAL

Vazquez, José L. "The Demographic Evolution of Puerto Rico and Its Transfer Value for Other Underdeveloped Areas." Doctoral dissertation, University of Chicago, Chicago, Illinois, 1964.

Index